Revolutionary Spirit

Exploring the Astrological Uranus

Haydn Paul was born in 1952, and lives near Leicester with his wife and three children. He has spent many years exploring the transpersonal way, and has been a practising Astrologer for over ten years.

REVOLUTIONARY SPIRIT

EXPLORING THE ASTROLOGICAL URANUS

Haydn Paul

ELEMENT BOOKS

First published in 1989 by
Element Books Limited
Longmead, Shaftesbury, Dorset

Printed and bound in Great Britain by Billings,
Hylton Road, Worcester

Cover illustration by David A. Hardy

Design by Max Fairbrother

British Library Cataloguing in Publication Data
Paul, Haydn
Revolutionary spirit: exploring the astrological uranus
1. uranus. astrological aspects
I. title
133. 5'3

ISBN 1-85230-059-0

Contents

From Revolution . . .

Traditional astrologers believed that there were only seven planetary bodies in our solar system, which were responsible for determining man's fate. The original boundary planet was Saturn, which was often considered to be a malefic influence., especially through the Middle Ages and Renaissance periods.

The surprise scientific discovery of the first of the three transpersonal planets, Uranus, and now also comprising Neptune and Pluto, was the first of a progressive series of scientific revelations and revolutionary thinking that have already transformed the world since the late eighteenth century. This radical process promised to stimulate even greater change as the speed of current technological advance intensifies.

Whilst traditional Hindu Vedic astrologers have claimed that they knew of the existence of the seventh mystery planet (they excluded the Sun from the planetary collective), the emergence of Uranus certainly came as a shock to the western astrologers. Perhaps those that were more esoterically orientated, might have realised that the symbol of Saturn as 'Dweller on the Threshold' possibly indicated the likelihood that some mysterious god still lurked unseen beyond the Saturnian rings.

Uranus symbolised the further opening of the mysteries of the universe, a new dimension of space expanded human concepts of our solar system, whilst simultaneously opening a corresponding channel within our minds and collective culture. This book is an attempt to explore and examine the implications of Uranus, and the impact of this energy upon contemporary man and the future world society. It is a new step for mankind to take, as we stand poised ready to enter the new world, where the new dimensions of space that awaits our exploration is that of the transpersonal levels of reality.

It was with a home made telescope that William Herschel located the mystery planet in the constellation of Gemini, on that night of March 13th, 1781. Initially, he thought that he had seen a comet, but further investigation and study of the object eventually confirmed the fact that it was a previously unrecognised planet and a member of our solar system.

The first name given to this new planet had been suggested by Herschel. It was 'Georgium Sidus', 'Georgian Star' in honour of King George III of England and Hanover. This was a clever move by Herschel. The King was extremely flattered by his suggestions to name the new planet after him, especially as it was the first to be discovered for centuries. Herschel was rewarded by being raised to the status of Kings Astronomer, and with the award of a yearly royal grant meant that he could devote his time in pursuit of his love of astronomy. However, the name failed to impress the scientific community, and was not commonly accepted as suitable (nor was the suggestion to call it 'Herschel' which also seemed to lack something...) Eventually, the sequence of naming the planets after the Roman Gods was to follow. Uranus re-joined the pantheon of Gods from which he had been excluded for so long, since the usurping of power over his creation by his son Saturn-Kronos. Uranus was impatient to become involved again in the world, and was intent upon making his presence felt as quickly as possible. In fact, the shadow of his coming had already preceded his actual appearance on the world stage.

By 1781, the Western world was beginning to experience radical social transformation. The old order of local agricultural communities which were living under the authoritative power of the landowners, aristocracy and monarchy was slowing fragmenting. It was a historical period that would become the birth of our modern state and civilisation. The emergence of the 'Industrial Revolution' stimulated a new age of science and technology, which began to mechanize previously labour intensive forms of production, and attract the migration of country people towards the growth of factory work in the expanding townships. Scientific, intellectual and more rational approaches became more culturally dominant, and in many ways, the people of the western nations began to throw off those stagnating shackles of social traditions and restrictions of thought that the power of the churches still possessed over them.

A revolutionary spirit permeated the atmosphere, and the early impact of Uranus would find that the new world of America and the old order of France would be receptive and willing to embody the new spirit of the age.

There are several similarities between the situation in America and France, even though one was a new frontier and the other an old culture. Both states were ruled by authoritarian attitudes. The French laboured under the 'ancient regime' of traditional 'divine right of the kings' and also through historical association, the aristocrats and landowners. The new Americans - often British emigrants - were dominated by the English imperial sovereign power, which insisted upon the right to legislate and tax what they considered to be just another colony.

Uranus is often associated with stimulating those ideas which lie just under the surface of consciousness, so that they erupt suddenly into life with a transformative power and impact. The ideas which were circulating at that time were revised concepts of republicanism and new images and perceptions of 'man'. It could be considered that the iminent discovery of Uranus was casting a shadow which was simultaneously stimulating the development of these ideas through the western intellectuals of the time. This would create the immediate channel through which Uranus would announce its arrival, and serve as an indication of the 'message' that it was intending to reveal.

These fermenting ideas and ideologies were primarily founded upon intellectual levels, and concerned the 'natural rights of man' irrespective of social advantages of birth, class and heritage. The concepts of republicanism had been in existence since the time of the Renaissance in Italy, but had often been considered to fail due to human fallibility and inability to live up to those ideals; often such attempts to create a state republic had eventually resulted in the creation of an autocratic despotic ruler.

These mental ideologies and philosophies developed the concept that the world was to be viewed as the creation of human choice and action, rather than the prior perception that the world was as it was through divine will or mere chance. Essentially, it was a theory of an individual responsibility, and which through collective choice and action, we make the world in which we live. Thus a republic was only possible if the people considered the well-being of the whole ultimately more important than their personal desires. A good republican citizen was to be 'a man of virtue'. This is an early idea of the interdependence of life on earth, a realisation of which our modern world is still struggling to accept and choose to live by its implications.

Ideas of democracy emerged, where the state is governed by and for the people, with open elections where any man could offer himself to be a representative and spokesman for his electorate, irrespective of his class or inheritance. Obviously, these advanced libertarian ideals were in direct conflict with the establishment, as symbolised by the monarchy.

In America, reaction to the British imposition of legislative rule over the colonies became a broad uprising across both country and city. It was a new land, with new settlers who wanted freedom to govern themselves. It was essential to abolish the monarchy and rule of the upper classes, and to symbolically 'kill the king, in 1776'.

They understood that to accept the idea if independence was to confidentially state their belief that a free people could govern themselves. The ideas of democratic republicanism took root, and as a result of the war between America and Britain from 1775–1781, America broke free of the British yoke, and formed a Confederation of States until 1778.

On the 4th of July, 1778, the Founding Fathers met in Philadelphia, and established the American Constitution. They were now citizens of the United States of America. The ideals which were held up to the people as a guiding light were enshrined in legislation, designed to promote the rights of individuals to decide what personal happiness was for them, and right to pursue it. It was a social vision of self respect and equal rights which brought about changes in the thinking and language of the concept of human freedoms, asserting human liberties and challenging the assumption of power by traditional elites.

The seeds of the American declaration of independence are reflected by high ideals and faith in the intrinsic goodness of mankind. In that sense they reflect the more positive Uranian ideals applied in practice. In France, the direct clash with the ruling nobility was more traumatic, and displayed a more negative reaction to the vibrations of Uranian change.

The same ideas were circulating in France, and more people were encouraged to become more responsible and to assert their collective power. This was partly stimulated by nobles, clergy and judiciary and the wealthy who for reasons of their own interests wanted to instigate unrest in order to erode the power of the monarchy. It was a time when Rosicrucian and Masonic occult ideas were spreading, when Mesmer was revealing the potency of hypnotism, and revolutionary political clubs were forming. Within the social flux, disparate groups began to coalesce into a movement that generated its own unstoppable momentum.

By 1789, there were nationwide disturbances, and a general collapse of the royal administration. The Declaration of Rights on the 26th of August 1789 asserted that all men are free and equal in rights, and aimed to abolish social distinctions based on privilege, rights of property, opinion, beliefs, and stated that national laws should be based on the general will of the people. Effectively this signed the 'death warrant' of the monarchal and aristocratic autocracy.

The revolutionary spirit had been unleashed, but while America was fighting for its own autonomy, France was attempting to change its whole social structure virtually overnight. The task was too daunting. The speed and nature of the changes began to run rampant and out of control. The old order had been broken,. but there was still nothing firmly founded which could replace it, and be capable of acting as a focus for re-establishing some social stability.

The eruption of such powerful liberating ideas were too advanced to be successfully integrated into the French culture. As the civil administrations collapsed, and military forces began to revolt, attempts to form new authoritative bodies failed as social change was too rapid, and influential groups rose overnight into power, and fell the next day to other coup d'etats. It became a negative anarchy, where in the urge to lay foundations for the future, the present was ignored, and so whatever was temporarily constructed was on a shifting sand which was continually moving. The attempt to elevate anarchy into a form of republican government also failed. Religion became a target for some, and anti-clerics began a process of de-christianization, establishing their 'Cult of Reason' and a secular humanist attitude emerged for a while.

In the early stages of the French Revolution, idealistic pacifism was dominant, but under the pressure of social change, and the power struggles between sects competing for power, the social fabric collapses even further, leading to the 'Great Terror'. The guillotine became more active, the symbol of chaos in France. The nobility and monarchy were permanently removed from their positions of power and social potency. The upholders of the Saturn social order were receiving the vengeance of a released Uranus. From the 22nd of September 1792, year 1 commenced in the republican calendar. A new birth, a new order, a new state.

The Uranian vision at work in the world was synthesised under the banner of 'Liberty, Equality and Fraternity', the conceptual seed of a new social relationship. The people had been possessed by the numinous quality of intellectual ideas of the time. It is of value to consider these initial impacts of Uranus upon receptive societies, because there is a clarity and purity of nature of this energy being revealed through these idealistic struggles for liberty and freedoms. It is an ongoing struggle in all areas of our contemporary world, either to try and preserve advances made, or even to start to embody them within a society.

That period of the late eighteenth century is a nursery of the modern world. There is a recognisable pattern that the ideas and social forces which took root in the world at that time, are still trying to push themselves into the world. The Uranian vision is still to be experienced. 1781 saw the first major outpouring of the concept of a 'Universal Brotherhood'. The two important revolutions of that period are related to becoming free from the bondage of matter (through scientific engineering progress in building productive machines, forms of mechanical transport and to eventually to today's electronic technology) and the concept of human rights and freedoms.

After successive advances which saw the harnessing of electro-magnetic forces, the growth in communicative abilities through air travel, cars, radio, TV, computers and global communication networks which can instantly disseminate information through messages transmitted through the air, we enter the world of Uranus. The direction that we are moving towards is that of the global mind-brain. To facilitate this journey, we also need to explore the nature of our own minds, so that we can participate with Uranus as co-creators of a 'world republic'.

CHAPTER 1

The Uranus Myths

THE MYTHS WHICH ARE ASSOCIATED with Uranus appear to operate within two distinct dimensions. One is the development of a cosmological theory, created by man attempting to explain the birth of the universe; and the second is related to the birth of the anthropomorphic gods, with their human-style marriages and family conflicts.

The cosmological theory reflects the belief that before the universe existed there was Chaos. This was the formless plenum void, the unmanifested, unconditioned abyss from which the birth of the cosmos would evolve. Chaos is the transcendent 'God-Head' beyond the physical universe.

From the permanent 'deep dark night' of Chaos, life and consciousness began to stir. In Greek myth, Ouranos became the First God, the one who was responsible for engendering the universe.

It was an overflowing of the latent creative potency within Chaos that erupted into the form of the cosmic Uranus principle. This is Uranus as a reflector of the 'Mind of God', where imagination and visualisation are capable of forming a spontaneously manifested creation. In the depths of the dream, there was the idea of a universe, and the universe was born.

In the original creation, ideation was sufficient to fertilise and unfold a universe which was still close to the unconditioned state of Chaos. The Bible refers to this creative spontaneity in Genesis, with the command 'Let there be Light'.

In Roman mythology, Ouranos became Uranus, the ancient god of the heavens and the sky. He was a male god, associated with the element of Air, and his divine ideas circulated in the heavenly mind, where the patterns of ideas whose time was still to come existed only as potential order.

There is some confusion concerning the relationship between Chaos and Uranus. Some sources suggest that Uranus was the grandson of Chaos, and was also the husband of his mother Gaia, who exists both as a cosmic womb and feminine principle and in a more restricted sense as 'Mother Earth'. This tends to suggest that Gaia is the daughter of Chaos, and is the primordial womb which gives birth to Uranus.

What is definite, however, is the 'marriage' between Uranus and Gaia, of Air and Earth. This symbolises the relationship between the unmanifest idea and the manifested limited form, the earthing of a vision.

Eventually there began to be elemental conflicts within this marriage. Uranus was preoccupied with his role as the dreaming creative mind, imagining beautiful ideas to pour into the universe, building great crystal castles in the sky. His imagination soared free in his universe of mind, unrestricted by mundane concerns.

On his irregular descents to fertilise Gaia with the seeds of his latest ideas for future developments, he was shocked to realise what he was actually creating in union with the Earth. His beautiful visions had given birth to what he perceived as monsters. The process of anchoring his dreams within the constraints of matter had created a progeny that he could not accept. These children, known as the Cyclopes and Titans were too ugly and encrusted in earthly vibrations to be his true children. Uranus rejected them and denied his fatherhood. He had seen his beautiful ideals tainted, and in his disappointment he banished them into the depths of Tartarus, which was a gloomy dark realm in the underworld hidden in the body of Gaia.

Gaia was, however, quite willing to accept her own children; after all, they were clothed in earthy matter like herself, and so their ugliness was only perceived by Uranus. Having them returned back to the 'womb' as failures began to be a strain, however. It was unnatural. She began to demand that the Titans – her children – take revenge upon their father. The Titans were reflections of emerging separate nature powers, and included Rhea, Okeanos and Kronos.

This was the first 'Battle of the Gods', where the new gods (as represented by the Titans) attempted to overthrow and usurp the power of the old (Uranus). Kronos was the Titan who listened to the begging of Gaia to take action against Uranus.

As Uranus approached Gaia, Kronos was waiting. He grasped the genitals of Uranus with his left hand (which would become the hand of ill omen), and with a curved sword or flint sickle castrated his father, throwing the severed genitals away into the ocean.

This myth has several levels of interpretation, similar to the way that it interpenetrates levels of reality, from cosmic theories to human conflicts. Uranus representing unconditioned time (timeless eternity) as the initial manifestation from Chaos, had lost his power as a result of his castration. The universe of infinity, the playground of the divine mind, had suddenly become finite, under the power of conditioning time as represented by Kronos.

Kronos now became the powerful god in time. Uranus had lost his creative potency, and could not spontaneously create through will, because he had lost his channel through which his idea-seeds could fertilise matter. Uranus had 'fallen from grace', and was no longer the ruler of this universe now dominated by matter (Earth–Gaia). He had been condemned to an existence of relative impotence as an outsider.

The unity and wholeness of the universe had been disrupted, and became restricted by time and space limitations, where life could only develop within circumscribed parameters. This is Kronos as symbolised by Saturn in astrological terms; the definer of boundaries, ring-pass-nots, imposing the power of rhythmic time patterns upon all of nature. The rebellion of the New Gods was successful, but at a cost to the freedom of the creation. The new dominance of the heavier vibration of matter over the light vibration of spirit occurs as a result of the battle.

This theme of rebellion is a recurring one. Amongst the progeny of Kronos (who was reputed to have followed almost in the footsteps of his father Uranus and tried to devour all his children at birth) was Zeus or Jupiter, who would eventually overthrow the rule of Kronos. It is the ongoing natural struggle between the old and the new, and the integration of new ideas into established patterns within life and consciousness, which is the underlying thematic story of evolution.

The act of castration is crucial, as it prohibited spontaneous creation through the power of the willed visionary mind, and replaced it with a reliance upon physical-plane procreative activity. This symbolises the descent into matter of the involutionary arc of spirit, imprisoned by the limitations of Kronos-Time. From another perspective, Uranus the Mind Dreamer became lost within his own dream.

The myth of the impotence and sterility of Uranus is reflected in the much later drama of the Grail Quest, in the symbol of the Maimed King. The King has been wounded in the genitals, and presides over the Waste Land. Here we see the ancient association of the vitality of the king with that of the land: if the king is not physically whole, then the land also becomes diseased through a lack of unity. Through losing his seed potency, the land enters a phase of decline and degeneration, and the Maimed King is forced to wait in frustration for the successful Grail Knight to heal him and free him from his suffering.

In the individual natal chart, these Grail themes are repeated. The house position of Uranus indicates through which area of life the revitalising new energy will be released, while the house position of Pluto indicates where this festering wound or obstacle is felt (see *Phoenix Rising: Exploring the Astrological Pluto*, Element Books, for a more in-depth analysis of this 'wound'). Finally, the position of Neptune indicates the healing nature of the Chalice, the mystical vision that heals through the experience of integration and unity.

An approach to this can be indicated through a chart which has, for example, Uranus in the 5th house, Pluto in the 6th, and Neptune in the 8th. Natal aspects include Uranus–Neptune square, and Neptune–Pluto sextile.

The 6th house Pluto leads to a deep dissatisfaction and disquiet in the spheres of work and service, where the individual feels very intensely that the lifestyle in this area is not suitable for his 'purpose' in life. He is experiencing a lack of meaning, and it feels like a literal wasteland of his energies and talents. It is like a living wound, a frustrating, seemingly insurmountable obstacle.

Neptune in the 8th house reveals the potential of a mystical death-and-rebirth process occurring, where he could experience the regenerative rising of the Phoenix within him. This is the point of inner healing, resolving a lack of integration into a more inclusive consciousness of unity. From the struggle to achieve a higher integration using the energies of the sextile between Neptune and Pluto, there is the potential to heal that Plutonic wound. If successful, the beneficial results can then flow out into a more fulfilling creativity through the 5th house Uranus, eventually building towards a more suitable work-service lifestyle, which simultaneously liberates and channels the previously unreleased energy in the 6th house. The transformation of the use of the mind through the Neptune–Pluto sextile, via a mystical inner rebirth, then dissolves the frustrating inner challenge of the Uranus–Neptune square, opening up the new horizons of Uranus.

It is significant that one eventual result of the emasculation of Uranus, led to the emergence of Aphrodite-Venus, who rose out of the sea in which Kronos had tossed the discarded genitals. This aspect of the myth implies that it was only through the transformation from a masculine principle through neutering and into a re-emergence as a watery love goddess that Uranus could regain a foothold in the Kronos-dominated universe. It could be commented that the seductive nature of Uranus-Aphrodite/Venus would lead a bewitched humanity towards the beckoning call of the transpersonal gods, through love, which opens us up to the unknown, and which helps to dissolve separatist barriers within ourselves and between us and others.

Parallel to these multi-levelled myths, we can see reflections within human societies of the polarised conflicts between matriarchal and patriarchal state attitudes and beliefs. The stories of elemental strife between the functions of Air and Earth, spirit and matter find resonance within the dominating social archetypes. Currently, we live within a patriarchal society, where men are the social leaders and *primes inter pares* – first amongst equals. Mind, reason and logic are the conditioning qualities, as well as belligerence and scientific objectivity.

The power of the masculine principle is paramount and has been so for over two thousand years. Since the time of the Greeks, when the myths were articulated, the 'sceptre of rulership' had been passed from the First Sky Father, Uranus, to Kronos-Saturn, reflecting the dominance of the patriarchal age.

Assertion, extroverted aggression, exploration and world dominion were followed under this masculine force, as a reaction to the even earlier matriarchal societies, where the rule of the divine feminine was powerful. Those were the times of the Earth Mother cults of the goddess Gaia, and the images of womanhood being worshipped.

The more transcendent conception of Uranus is similar to that of the Hindu god Varuna, who was envisaged as the encompasser of the universe, infinite space, who manifested all life from the power of his seed, and from whom the paradox of the 'everything from nothing' emerges.

Meanwhile, the Greeks attempted to bring Uranus down to earth, where according to Diodorus, he was the first king of fabled Atlantis, which was the land where the gods had their birth. This king was their Sky Father-God, and the first teacher of the science of astronomy; even then he was pointing towards the heavens.

The modern task of Uranus is to regain friendly terms with Gaia. Now that mankind has developed to this stage, it is inimical to future growth for the First God to remain aloof above his creation, brooding over the mistakes and suffering of the past. We have to draw him through again so that a living relationship with the Divine Mind can be re-established; cross-fertilisation is necessary for the next steps forward.

Yet this will have to become a new relationship of reconciliation between earth and air, matter and spirit, within ourselves and in the larger society. We can become the point of reconciliation (the trine) between Uranus and Gaia, resolving those opposing energies. What does this mean? What does it imply in individual and social terms? An attempt to explore this will be made in Chapters 3 and 8.

The astrological Uranus is currently perceived as being perpetually engaged in the struggle with Saturn-Kronos, aiming to break restricting barriers and to offer the freedom of new expansionary opportunities. This battle of the gods is an innate living pattern in our own personalities, a conflict that we experience throughout life. In this sense, Uranus is attempting to regain some influence over the world of Kronos, to begin to redirect it once again towards his vision of creative mental freedom of ideas and ideals. Yet because he is so distant from us, and his potential impact is so great, he can only communicate in sudden erratic bursts of inspiration or through crisis creating sudden change. The relatively recent 'rebirth' of the Uranian principles during the late eighteenth century appears to indicate that the world is now ready for the fresh vitalisation of the Uranus energy. It is an energy which can begin to liberate us from the confines of absorption within matter, pointing us towards the liberation of mind and the exploration of the Sky-Father's heavens.

It is time for us to reintegrate Uranus into our nature, to move beyond our identification with the Kronos-Saturn domination of earth and matter. The quest for the way to the mountaintop will offer new ways of perceiving ourselves and the world, and the higher vision will begin to merge again with the futuristic ideals and plans of the cosmic Uranus. Uranus expects us to become his new channel of communication with the world, to 'replace his severed genitals' and become his creative agents for change. The interpenetration of the timeless and time will again occur and a breakthrough into a new dimension of reality can be made. This will be when a new perception of the nature of time and cycles of existence is understood and integrated into human knowledge. Contemporary astrology, with its investigations into cyclic patterns within human nature and society, is one source for such new enquiries.

CHAPTER 2

Reflecting the Astrological Uranus

URANUS WAS THE FIRST OF the transpersonal planets to be scientifically discovered, and is the nearest of the three to the Earth. The other two planets of this transcendent trinity are Neptune and Pluto. These three are the planets which astrologically are related to civilisational and cultural developments, where transformative change sweeps across generations and societies.

These trans-Saturnian planets have a collective effect, stimulating activity within the collective unconscious level of mind. The individuals capable of registering and responding to these high vibrational energies are those who are progressive thinkers, artists of various kinds, or those engaged in self-exploration and spiritual enquiry. This is because these are the individuals who have opened up conscious channels capable of accessing their unconscious levels of mind in order to receive inspiration, and who act as channelling 'mediums' for the evolutionary forces to enter humanity. From this group emerge the new scientific revelations and technological developments; the new forms and contents of artistic, literary and musical expressions that reflect inner movement in the collective mind of society; new approaches to political theory and governmental directions; and new spiritual impulses which reflect a religious impetus or offer techniques of inner personal development.

Even within this more responsive world group, there can be difficulties in assimilating and applying the energies of the transpersonal planets. There is often a characteristic of unique individuality and what some consider to be eccentricity associated with such people, and sometimes a lack of balance due to an obsessiveness in some sphere of life. And yet these people are the creative channels who make a lasting mark upon society, recorded in history for their contribution to humanity.

The majority of humanity barely recognises the influence of these stimulatory energies in their individual and collective lives. They do not hear the inspiring whispers of the artistic muses; or feel that insatiable curiosity of the scientific mind to penetrate, dissect, analyse and understand the workings of man and the universe; or that need to become a leader of men; or the longing to feel at one with life that tugs at the heart of the mystic, aiming to dissolve that sense of isolating separation.

For most people, Uranus, Neptune and Pluto act as 'fates'. As these energies often fail to be consciously integrated in people's lives, their influence can only be released through 'acts of destiny', in situations that appear to be beyond personal control, and are imposed by the 'outer world'. Phases of crisis occur, where as a result of previous choices, the individual enters the period of reaping whatever he has sown in life. Often these are felt as constrained choices, where options are severely limited, or where inner personality patterns create a sense of `I didn't have any choice ...' as though that is a satisfactory answer or excuse for the resulting consequences. 'I couldn't help myself ...' is another favourite of the individual who is living a basically unconscious life.

Beyond the more immediate effects of personal choices are the political decisions made by a ruling elite (with the deliberate or tacit and passive approval of the people), which have a direct influence upon the nature of the individual life and freedom. Wars, civil unrest and problems of economic survival seem to be beyond the scope of influence of most people, but in the last analysis, in the West we elect our leaders and give them our personal power. Social and political leaders who are elected, embody a majority viewpoint in some psychological way. If we are asleep, and separatist attitudes are dominating, then the only leaders that we can elect are those who reflect our own prejudices and unconscious attitudes. After all, individuals create the group collective; the current expression of a national society is the result of previous individuals and our present attitudes. If we do not like it, then it is our right and obligation to begin to change the world in which we live. Turning a 'blind eye', and pretending that it is not our responsibility is a denial of our real individual creative power, which is then grasped by less scrupulous characters, who succeed in gaining power and proceed to inflict their separatist policies upon us. And then as 'the fates' affect our lives, we curse destiny for what it is doing to us. We have done it to ourselves; it has been our choice to give power to such as Hitler. Our 'fate' has been the result of our own choices.

This is, in fact, a major Uranian theme. From the time of the mythological Uranus, who chose to imprison his children out of sight because they failed to match his ideals, he created the eventual revolt from Gaia and Kronos. His choice became his fate. It was the first social revolution, the overthrowing of a negative rulership by the resistance of the subjects. Ever since then, Uranus has been transformed into a revolutionary, perpetually engaged in attempts to regain his throne by shattering the boundaries imposed by Kronos-Saturn upon the human life.

The Uranus-Saturn polarity is a key to understanding the effect of the Uranus energy upon humanity, and within the individual. In a simplistic sense, it is the conflict between the forces of order (Saturn), and the forces of chaos (Uranus), between the known and the unknown. What is interesting is this association of Uranus with chaos, disruption and rebellion. Obviously, Uranus is a child of the original Chaos – the unconditioned creative power – and thus 'genetically' has the nature of that energy firmly embedded in the Uranus vibration. Yet even in the myth, the initial intention of Uranus was to create a beautiful universe from the power of his imagination, which implies a structuring and ordering principle at work, where the unconditioned universal flux begins to be shaped into artistic patterns by a master craftsman attempting to manifest his vision. So it could be said that the Uranus energy has a vibratory quality of chaos-order, with the real purpose being to impose order upon dissipated free-flowing energy. We will see this theme amplified in Chapter 7.

The Saturn principle, the child Kronos, had 'genetically' absorbed the pattern of order from his father, and this overshadowed the liberating chaotic quality, which had in fact been denied and repressed. Thus Saturn has to define, to impose structures and boundaries, through creating ring-pass-nots in the struggle to limit and contain the expansive inner nature of the creation. Saturn has become identified with restriction and caution, stability and security, denying the soaring of the creative imagination and the urge for new horizons. Through the conditioning factor of time in the human life, Saturn restrains those transpersonal energies which shatter all restrictions of mind and body. This does have a real value though, in that it forces growth and maturation to occur, rather than a dangerous rush towards the new with little or no understanding of the forces that can be unwittingly unleashed. Under the pressures of World War II, mankind opened the doorway to atomic energy before the likely consequences were understood. Once the right inner state is reached, then the inhibiting door dissolves naturally, and the new horizons can be safely approached.

It is the ongoing interaction and perpetual opposition between Saturn and Uranus that is the prime factor in the socialisation of humanity, caught between the process of involution and evolution, through the midpoint of revolutionary change. Uranus disrupts patterns of stability and shatters a stagnating status quo, both within society and within the individual. The French, American and Russian Revolutions are evidence of this activity.

The Uranian function is to act as the stimulatory agent ushering life beyond whatever barriers have been erected by Saturn; he is the first siren call from the beyond, using the revolutionary process to create his purpose of transformation in the world. As with the effects of Pluto, the initial impact can be confusing, bewildering and painful as Uranus takes the society or individual beyond the security of the known familiar world away from the domination of Saturn. The potentiality and newness of a greater world is then displayed, and offered to the brave explorer. This expansive world has always been there, but the influence of Saturn as experienced through social conditioning (education, religion, national cultures, etc.) has blinkered the mind. These shocking new horizons had never even been imagined before, let alone experienced. The old foundations are swept away by the impact. This can be one of the problems of Uranian receptivity, where there is no value given to the past amidst the overwhelming enthusiasm for future possibilities. It is better to integrate the best of the existing social structures into the new order, modifying where necessary, learning from the past rather than rejecting it outright.

Such Uranus activity may coincide, through transit or progression, with the inner arousal of a sense of discontent with the established pattern of the individual life. The repetitive nature of a conventional life can begin to feel uncomfortably restrictive, and the urge to break free of the imprisoning bonds can become extremely powerful. The Uranian impulse is one of rebellion arising from a personal need to be independent and break with convention, throwing off personality shackles and being reborn as a new person, unencumbered by old patterns. This can create the opportunity for a previously unrecognised persona to emerge, one which has always been hidden within an efficient organised and disciplined individual. Much as the butterfly emerges from the shielding cocoon of its chrysalis, so a 'new individual' can erupt into social life. `I never knew he/she had it in them ...' is a common response to such a change occurring within a friend or relative. Yet it has always been there, as a potential, probably recognised by the individual but denied expression.

It is a leap towards freedom, a demand for freedom, an essential movement towards an individual uniqueness, a search for an inner guiding light pointing towards a waiting destiny: this is what allows change to happen.

This can be a fated unconscious change occurring without apparent volition, imposed by an impersonal world; or it can be a conscious choice, willingly accepted and co-operated with by a person who acknowledges the need for inner transformation. The ways in which this force can manifest are many, and can include a sudden realisation that one has outgrown one's current lifestyle, a need to change employment, or leaving an unsatisfactory relationship behind. There may be sudden flashes of insight as if a lightning bolt had just illuminated your inner mind and nature, allowing a greater degree of self-perception and understanding. There may be new ideas, philosophical or religious concepts that offer a new direction in your life. The result is the dismantling of the existing life pattern, prior to reassembly in a more suitable form. If there is resistance, then it will create more suffering and instability until you are forced to accept change, probably by the decisions of others leaving you no choice but to bow to the inevitable.

For some, the activity of Uranus is a thrilling experience. These are those who have already accepted the nature of this planet, perhaps because they have a strong Uranian influence in their natal charts and have had previous experience of its potency. These are the natural revolutionaries, forward-looking positive thinkers (as opposed to the past-orientated reactionaries more naturally attuned to Saturn), who perceive the black hole of the future as a land of opportunity and creative space, and not something to resist through fear.

There is an electric rapidity to the Uranus vibration that is especially attractive to the intellectual, and to those who get bored without a continual supply of fresh mental stimuli. It can amplify and quicken rational thought so that it resembles intuitional insight, thus forming new patterns of understanding, and it enhances the ability to synthesise information into unifying holistic structures. A psychic sensitivity can be increased, expanding the boundaries of individual receptivity to include previously unexplored areas of human knowledge.

This urge to discover can even lead into the traditional sphere of the mystic, where the inner illumination reveals the illusions of dualistic thinking. It is a holistic universe that is perceived, where the confines of an attitude of mind which differentiates into antagonistic opposites are shattered, and are replaced by a higher mind which unifies through an understanding of the complementary nature of the dualities. Here the 'either-or' dichotomy is resolved, and a natural balance of mind is restored through a dissolution of the conflictual lower mind.

The Uranus energy may be experienced in its positive and negative forms, often simultaneously. This poses a problem to the individual's absorption of the energy, and is often unbalancing. The individual may become temperamental, highly strung, nervy, swinging between extremes of attitude and behaviour. There may be an unsettling vibration in the mind-body aura which can be disturbing and unpleasant for others, and can eventually lead to social isolation.

The activity of Uranus often causes problems in relationships, echoing the mythological relationship between Uranus and Gaia. A strong Uranus-Aquarian-Air influence within the natal chart implies a focus on the mental level. Here, common characteristics can include an impersonal manner, detachment, objectivity, a lack of human warmth and a preference for cool rationality and logical intellectual pursuits. A denial and rejection of the intangible, disruptive emotional/feeling empathic level is often displayed. The need for freedom from commitments and responsibilities is common, as well as that niggling belief that a more exciting relationship could be found with somebody new, or that an affair could enliven a dull, predictable life. The Uranus energy is always looking for the exit, so that if it needs to move quickly, it knows the way out! The problem is that this does not lead to a stable relationship, which is what the majority of people really want. A succession of temporary intimate relationships over the span of an adult life rarely satisfies.

It may be envied by some, who would love to taste that freedom and 'forbidden fruit' once again, but for the participant there is a sense of disillusionment and failure, a recognition of the fickleness of human nature, always seeking, never satisfied. In the more bohemian, unconventional life styles of many who are responsive to Uranus, the end result may be a multiplicity of fragmented relationships with no unifying cohesiveness, except an urge for free experimentation and superficial emotional exploration, a dissipated life, strewn with the threads of unfinished business.

It is undeniable that Uranus stimulates unorthodox relationships. How the individual deals with this influence can depend on the environment in which they live.

They may have a lifestyle that offers opportunity for change and novelty to be experienced, thus providing the energy with a means of release. However, if the home situation is repressive, perhaps through an authoritarian spouse, a younger family, or financial pressures, then there is unlikely to be a suitable channel for the energy to work through. It can become distorted, and hidden inner pressure can build, until it erupts through relationship friction, or the dam walls break, shattering the existing life pattern and the marriage collapses, or the security of a job is left.

There is a feeling of a need to be free from commitment and responsibility, a feeling of being restricted from following some 'great destiny' by the demands of the family. The challenge is to balance this urge with the acceptance and fulfilling of all social obligations. It can be a difficult balance to achieve and maintain.

The Uranian rebel resents and will try to resist the imposition of any manipulative social boundaries in order to discover a state of freedom. He is rarely the company man, or the ideal marriage partner, unless the changeable, inquisitive, erratic searcher is what you need as a stimulant to develop. Uranus-Air may work quite well with a dominating Fire partner, but an association with a powerful Earth or Water type is likely to lead to conflict sooner rather than later!

In the sexual aspect of intimate relationships, traditional astrology often associates Uranus with experimentation, deviancy or perversion. This may reflect the contemporary confusion over what constitutes orthodox or unorthodox sexual behaviour. This behavioural definition varies from one society to another according to cultural or religious teachings, and so there is probably no real norm of activity across the world, just a variety of either majority or minority preferences.

A Uranian attitude to this issue is to allow freedom for each to find their own adult preferences, and to allow their exploration of them. A slightly less extreme Uranian attitude would be to qualify this with the proviso that other individuals should not in any way be harmed by the expression of such sexual freedom. Thus, child pornography and abuse, or sexual violence, for example, would not be socially acceptable, and would be liable to penalisation.

The more traditional connection of Uranus with homosexuality can be perceived in terms of 'chosen impotency' on the physical plane of human procreation through an emotional choice of a same-sex partner, but does not deny the expression of potential creativity through the artistic or scientific intellect. Many famous artists and scientific minds have been homosexual, and have greatly contributed to human progress. At this time, the question of whether homosexuality is 'natural or a deviancy' is still open to debate. Until mankind unfolds and explores the future androgynous state, and understands that nature of dualistic polarities on earth, then any answer to that question remains one of personal bias. A Uranian attitude would consider such a question for debate to be irrelevant in any evaluation of a person.

Certainly, whether within heterosexual or homosexual relationships, Uranus tends towards promiscuity, curiosity and a desire for new experiences. The Uranus-Venus/Aphrodite association can be a fertile ground for the impulse of change in a static life. Sudden affairs embarked upon by either partner can create the upheaval which causes a need for a complete rethinking and review of the lifestyle and choices made.

If Uranus makes harmonious aspects with other planets (trine, sextile), then it is likely that the sexual expression will basically conform to socially acceptable and traditional practices, although an element of mutual experimentation will be looked for in relationships. If the aspects are more challenging (square, opposition and probably the conjunction too), then there will be more inner pressure to move beyond the conventional norm, and a more complex sexuality may emerge. If aspects are made between Uranus and the Sun, Mars or Jupiter, then these more expansionary extroverted masculine energies can build an extremely strong sexual drive, almost obsessional and offering powerful sexual experiences especially at times when the Uranus vibration is 'switched on'. When Uranus is in aspect with the more feminine planets like Venus and the Moon, there will be an emphasis placed upon the values of sensitivity, but the Uranus energy will emerge through attractions to unconventional relationships, perhaps promiscuity and a lack of commitment and emotional involvement in love affairs. With either group of aspects, jealousy will be hated, and attempts at emotional smothering will be rejected or resisted. The need to feel free and independent will never be subdued even within a marriage; in fact it is often within that commitment that an awareness arises of how deep that need actually is, and how foolish it would be to repress or deny its existence.

URANUS AND HEALTH

A highly energised Uranus energy can be a considerable influence upon the functioning of the physical body. This is because the quality of the energy has an electrical nature, operating on the level of mind and through the sympathetic nervous system. As this energy flows erratically and intermittently into these receptive channels, the pressure placed on the capacity of·the circuits to cope with the higher voltage may cause stress and tension.

The problem for an individual who is either highly receptive to this energy (through several Uranus aspects for example), or for one who cannot easily absorb and integrate this vibration into their lives (through a strong Earth pattern, Saturn limitations or even excessive Water associations), is the degree to which their minds and nervous system are suddenly 'charged up'.

In the first case, of the receptive person, there is the pressure to change, a flooding of new ideas, opportunities, desires for experimentation and new horizons that offer a challenge of choice and selection, along with the experience of a disturbing and disruptive vibration. The question is how to control and focus this, so that the energy is released safely into creative channels which allow the tension to be dissolved, whilst still allowing new opportunities to be pursued.

In the second case, of a person whose astrological emphasis is primarily resistant to the Uranus energy, there is likely to be a build-up of denied impulses, with a clinging to established routine and the status quo. The challenge here involves being able to allow a slow and relatively controlled change to proceed, which could mitigate the inner need for a more radical restructuring of the whole life.

Irrespective of any personal response, Uranus will not be ignored or denied. If the energy is not channelled, nervous illness may arise, as the Uranus stimulus swamps the resistance and natural neuro-circuit capacity of the individual. Certainly there are many in the West who suffer from 'nervous problems', or who have to take tranquillisers in order to cope with life. Possibly the relatively recent increase in receptivity to Uranus is amplifying this problem, as the influence of this energy grows ever stronger within the collective unconscious mind, and reveals itself by erupting through such illnesses.

There are several associated nervous-physical effects, such as body spasms, convulsions, heart palpitations and even paralysis, which may be connected to the i regular electrical charges transmitted via the nervous system.

It could be worthwhile to consider the natal chart of an individual suffering from nervous problems in the light of Uranus activity, evaluating their likely receptivity and response to its impact. Possibly some self-exploration and therapy could help them to discover an approach to personal transformation which enables them to absorb the energies more easily, and to use them in a more creative manner. The whole area of physical well-being and the astrological associations is obviously one that potentially offers considerable insight and value.

Uranus is also linked with the endocrine system, which is a system of ductless glands which secrete chemicals into the blood, aiding efficient bodily functions.

Major glands in this system can be linked to the seven major etheric energy chakras of yoga and occult paths. The two glands that Uranus is often associated with are the gonads and the pineal.

The gonads are the 'sex glands' of the endocrine system, and are the physical-plane counterpart of the sacral chakra. This is the sphere of physical reproduction and human creativity as a natural biological function, and represents the manifestation principle at work. Uranus is often associated with homosexuality. If this is a valid connection, any such tendencies in the individual will depend on the placing of Uranus by house and aspect.

It may be more useful to perceive the gonads-sacral centre as the lower pole of an alignment with the other head gland of the pineal. The pineal is linked with the head chakra, the 'Thousand Petalled

Lotus' of the yogic path, and with the later stages of the spiritual way towards union. It is only awakened as the focus of the inner energies is transferred from the lower centres to the higher centres of the head. The pineal is sometimes considered to be the 'third eye', or the 'seat of the soul'. This is the realm of the intuition, accessing the universal mind, creating the inspired creative visionary, the occult initiate or master.

This is reminiscent of the mythological Uranus, the creator by imagination and directed thought (the pineal-head centres), and the physical level manifestation (the gonads-sacral creative repro-duction). There is a link connecting these centres, which again is surely concerned with the mysteries of sexuality, which are also related to the science of union and the relation of spirit and matter. This is a noticeable theme threading through these explorations of Uranus.

A final idea, which may be capable of further exploration, is the concept of Uranus as a force striving to break free into independ-ence from the confines of a rigidly controlling structure. Relating this to the human body, with its clearly defined organic boundaries and functions, which is mentally identified as a separate individual (an isolated island in the universe), could suggest the process of cancer occurring in the cells of the body. The local area of a cancer can be associated with an adjacent energy centre, which by impli-cation is probably being overstimulated through the glandular and nervous systems. This symbolises the sphere of life which is being inhibited and repressed, thus creating a blockage and build-up of unexpressed energy, which then causes the body cells to 'revolt' and strive for an independent existence – in the form of malignant tumours. Often cancer is triggered by emotional suppression, but it could also be related to the Saturn-Uranus conflict, whereby the urge to break fixed boundaries and expand into a new way of life is repressed.

REFLECTING URANIAN PERSONALITIES

These are a few scattered observations about Uranian-type 'friends'. For reasons of anonymity, and to protect all those whom they fit, no identifying names will be used, except the sobriquet 'our friend'.

Our friend will always assert their unique individuality, elevating this into a personal necessity (or excuse) to remain free and uncommitted, detached and uninvolved. Free to explore where and when and with whoever they choose. Refuses to be bound, even by emotional or family obligations. Watch the straining at the leash to be free.

Our friend is eccentric; watch that mind sparking off as if electric charge detonations were exploding in the head. Shame that nothing ever comes of these ideas, or that projects are never finished because the next one is always more fascinating. Tense? Don't touch or else you'll get a shock!

Our friend is unconventional, lives the life that he wants to, even if it means travelling in the opposite direction to everyone else. Takes great delight in breaking all the social rules, it confirms the unconventionality, and also gives great ego gratification.

Our friend is a weirdo, doesn't fit into anything, lives in a world alone, because being so far gone is way outside normal society. Some say our friend is a sexual deviant, but he never seems to have any opportunities.

Our friend believes in universal brotherhood. A friend to all, who proposes great liberal reforms offering freedom to everyone, an altruist and humanitarian. The problem is, everybody becomes frightened at the thought of having to change.

Our friend is a seeker of the truth, a scientist, occultist, astrologer, inventor, is there no end to the insights and intuitions of this mad genius of mind? Shame he forgets about human emotions ... Our other friend is the anarchist. 'Who needs leaders?' he shouts to the group following him. The rebel whose arguing, dissenting, heretical thoughts are not suitable for family viewing. The freedom fighter challenging social establishments and traditions. But what would they be replaced by? Oh, not enough time to tell you that, it's time for the Revolution! But then he has a friend who is a 'positive anarchist' who has many ideas ... Another friend always joins groups, in order to find like minds and intelligent social conversation. Problem is that he soon leaves, because his individuality is not being 'stroked' in a group of like minds, where he becomes one of the crowd. And anyway, he's quite argumentative.

Do *you* recognise any of these traits in yourself or your friends?

CHAPTER 3

New Mansions of Mind

URANUS IS ASSOCIATED with the element of Air, and with a perception of life that is focused on the level of mind. Individuals who are attuned to Uranus have great mental curiosity and need for stimulation and excitement. They are impelled by a deep motivation to be future-orientated, innovative and destroyers of static life patterns.

During this century, there has been an explosion of scientific enquiry into the human mind and consciousness, human physiology and the brain. The results of these investigations have often paralleled and coalesced with those of quantum mechanics, and the investigative probing into the realities of the hidden microcosmic universe. Increasingly, the perceptual belief of a universe of 'solid matter' is dissolving as such research progresses; what is emerging – to the surprise of the scientists and physicists – is a universe that is much stranger than had previously been dreamt of by Western minds. If anything, what is being rediscovered through advanced technology is a universe that reflects the insights and images expressed by the mystics, shamans, yogis and occultists of the past. The Hindu concept that the world is 'maya' (a 'real illusion') and a 'lila' (a divine play and drama) becomes increasingly viable. The mystical experience that includes a sense of being drowned within a sea of light-waves closely fits with the real world of light and energy frequencies that underlies the common human reality. With the use of modern scientific instruments, it is into these levels of existence that the contemporary physicist is delving.

Sir Arthur Eddington commented early in this century that 'the stuff of the universe is mind-stuff'. The physicality of the universe is beginning to be recognised as being more illusory than was previously thought; even physicists are starting to regard it as a universe of mind, manifested on a possibly infinite variety of levels. As the earlier Theosophical teachings stated, spirit is matter vibrating at its highest frequency, and matter is spirit vibrating at its lowest frequency. The two are indivisible, and are really the one life and consciousness expressed as a perceptual polarity. This reflects Uranus the creator god, who formed the physical universe out of mind.

The revolutionary impulse of Uranus in the individual and the collective is recognised, but there are questions to be answered: Where does this impulse intend to lead us? What changes are demanded? What is the vision of the future that the Uranian Idea intends us to embody? What is the real revolution that is occurring? What is the future path?

We can begin to understand at least part of this evolutionary intention through self-exploration. We start with ourselves; we are the revolution. This is accepted on the more progressive levels of world culture and society: we alone can embody the messages of the 'New Age', as we are the mediators and transforming agents for the transpersonal energies. The point is that we are being asked to become conscious co-creators of the world in which we participate; it is a demand that we now take responsibility for our choices and actions, and begin to 're-design' our world to match the vision of reality that is being unfolded through science, the world of interdependence, Gaia, and spaceship Earth.

The key is relationship, an internal and external unifying contact. This key appears to lie within ourselves, hidden in our body–brain–mind structure. Brain research has discovered one reason why our mental outlook is primarily divisive in nature; it is because the physical structure of the brain is dualistic, having two separate hemispheres which have distinct and different functions.

The world can be loosely divided into East and West, the orient and the occident. This split reflects the dominating styles of perception and attitude of the respective social cultures. The East has tended to explore what is now known as the 'right brain', and the West has concentrated on the functions of the 'left brain'. These respective focuses have dictated the type of societies that have developed over time. Obviously, no society or culture expresses one hemisphere to the exclusion of the other, but one side becomes dominant and over-emphasised, conditioning the acceptable patterns of social thought.

The brain is a highly complex physical structure, and research is only at the early stages of identifying the mechanisms by which it operates and responds to stimuli. It is through the brain that the mind or consciousness activates the physical body; brain damage drastically impinges on the functioning of that body, restricting options of living and experience. Conversely, awakening the brain into greater activity could transform life into hitherto unsuspected expanded horizons. This potential is worth exploring, and is, I believe, a purpose of the overshadowing Idea of Uranus, especially when functioning as the hierophant and ruler of the occult path (see Chapter 7).

The brain hemispheres interact, but each has its own unique role and function to perform. In the West, we have activated the left-brain approach to life much more strongly than we have its partner, the right brain. What is needed is a rebalancing, a conscious effort to awaken the right-brain activity in our society. The signs are already present that Easterners are seriously applying left-brain attitudes in their industrial and economic developments, or at least duplicating the technological advances of the West.

The left brain is that of the analytical divisive mind, of logic, rationality, the spoken and written word, and number; it is the investigator of universal parts and fragments. Basically, we have been encouraged to identify ourselves with these left-brain associations, and socially have relatively few concepts of holistic relationships. Many people still look askance at ecological projects and any thinking which reflects perceptions of interdependence. The left brain identifies through separation, categorisation, placing into compartments, structure, organisation, measuring and naming processes. In many ways, it functions in a similar way to a computer database, in which information is stored through memory, and all new experience is compared with this database information and is categorised in terms of familiar established patterns. It has a predilection for tradition, as this enables it to function more easily, offering a recognisable process of relating to events. Experience is processed through this filter, identified according to established labelled recognition categories and stored for future reference. This helps to build our concept and belief in a separate self, named and distinct from everyone else, and to maintain the illusion of a static single self.

The right brain processes all the experience and information that the left brain cannot successfully link into the existing database of correspondences and associations. It is more concerned with feelings and emotional tones, artistic qualities, music, sexuality, symbols and images, and most importantly, the perception of context and holistic patterns of meaning and relatedness. The right brain seems to understand these patterns that it discerns in the information that it processes. It enjoys and responds easily to newness and the unknown, and it has an innate tendency to complete 'pictures of reality' forming new *Gestalten* of a unifying holistic pattern. Whilst the left brain dissects information, fitting it into preformed channels, the right brain works with this information, placing it in a holistic context. In several ways, the right hemisphere reflects 'heart' associations and tendencies, life reflected as feeling and responsive emotion, with changes in moods and altered states of consciousness. Seeing the universe from a right-brain perspective becomes a more direct and intense feeling experience, which results from being freed from the constraints and fragmenting filters of the left-brain perspective, which is attuned to the separatist mind.

It is interesting to note that even with this hemispherical distinction, parallels between the ongoing conflict of Uranus and Saturn are reflected by the right and left brains respectively. Modern humanistic astrology has been more concerned with unfolding right-brain insights in the reformulation of traditional predictive astrology towards a more psychologically founded approach. Astrology is a good example of the two approaches. There is the analytical and categorising data base of associations and probability tendencies derived from the nature of the planets, signs and houses involved, and there is the attempt to build a clarifying and unifying reflection of the whole individual and to explore the underlying impulses and archetypal patterns operating through him. Additionally, transpersonal astrology places individual development within a social, global and universal context, offering a holistic interpretation in which 'no man is an isolated island in the universe'. Astrology offers the potential to work with this dual brain processing, as it synthesises the two paths.

As Jung suggests, modern man is in search of his soul, looking for a sense of meaning and purpose in life, so that he can lift his sights above the mundane and merely trivial. The lack of meaning currently felt in the West is symptomatic of left-brain dominance.

In resolving our individual needs for integration and transformation, we are also engaged in a vitally necessary social task.

A new harmony needs to be achieved, which is a relational consciousness between the two hemispheres, enabling the mind to operate through a unified mechanism of the brain. This would give us a new unity and centre, a 'soul' from which we could direct and perceive life from a new level of understanding, healing inner fragmentation and personality splits and in so doing redefining the Self.

It has to be recognised that personal behaviour is primarily a result of social conditioning interacting with those intrinsic personality patterns that are reflected by the natal chart. This combination imposes a pattern of responses upon the brain, which then directs the individual functioning and defines the options of choice open to the individual. Yet these are not inviolable fixed patterns – even though they may seem so – but only condition a relatively plastic and mutable structure into predictable patterns of personal expression. What Uranus is seeking to achieve is the restructuring of the personality or society, an opening of new possibilities. It acts as an evolutionary impulse, implementing processes of re-programming, which can be consciously achieved as we will consider later.

The brain mathematically constructs our sense of a 'physical universal reality' out of frequencies received from a dimension that transcends time and space. All sensations are really frequencies of energy vibration which are the ground of the universe. The brain encounters these frequencies, processing the information coded into these vibrations and then interpreting it according to its inner database and preconceptions of reality. The universe that is experienced is thus not the real universe, but one which is a result of our brain-mind programme (which is primarily a consensual social construct, a joint agreement and heritage of a traditional view of life). The universe that we inhabit and experience is created by our own interpretation of free-flowing data. We are participants in reality, co-creators and observers who are interrelated and affect what we are observing (as the physicists have realised).

The dual nature of the brain leads to innate difficulties in dealing with conflicts which arise from apparently contradictory information; the paradoxical nature of a universe in which 'opposites' co-exist as complementary aspects of one whole poses a challenge which is normally evaded by repression or denial of the facts.

Unless an effective integration is made, the process of individual preferential choice interferes and the universe is seen through a partial mirror, which over time reflects only those aspects and experiences that are socially and personally acceptable.

But this is not an inevitable process. There are alternatives, and life is always full of them. Only closed, fragmented minds believe that there are no alternatives. Individually and collectively, we stand on the brink of a new stage in evolution, an opening of the hidden doors, whereby a transformative paradigm shift in our world views of self and other is ready to illuminate our way. Such shifts are part of the ongoing Uranian revolution, and occur periodically in human history; they are natural consequences of having passed certain 'landmarks' in human progression and make available powerful, inclusive ideas and discoveries to those who are receptive.

Paradigm shifts involve new ways of perception and understanding which explain our experiences of reality in a more accurate and satisfying manner. Often, they are initially rejected; the majority fail to comprehend them. Equally, those with vested interests may prefer to maintain the old social views, as the new can often destroy the foundations of their own beliefs or undermine their power over others. As a result, the knowledge implicit in these shifts remains in the possession of a progressive open-minded minority.

One trigger for such a shift in contemporary science was Einstein's breakthrough in the theories of relativity by 1905; this opened the door for future investigation into atomic science and quantum physics. Yet most of the implications of these changes have still to be absorbed by society, and within the average person's conception of the universe and their own role in it. Paradigm shifts create crises, similar to the Uranian individual revolutions as it transits through the houses; in fact, they are symptomatic of this same process at play, occurring primarily within the level of mind and consciousness, although having more material effects later in time. The new paradigm will include the knowledge and information of the paradigm that it is replacing, but it destroys those barriers of limitation and creates a more inclusive theory and explanation. It is a progression of that original realisation on a higher turn of the spiral, and such paradigm shifts occur in all spheres of human knowledge.

The shift that is considered here is that of the body-brain-mind continuum. Research is now demonstrating that psychotherapies and spiritual yogic/meditational/occult practices actually do lead to a deeper integration within physical brain functioning. What occurs over time, and as a result of personal experimentation, is an increased coherence and harmony in the brainwaves and hemispherical synchronisation. An enhanced degree of organisation and more efficient processing of sensory information also appears to occur within such practitioners, who are undergoing what will eventually become an accelerated movement towards transformation. Restructuring, reprogramming, or meta-programming are all terms to indicate this individual process of change; and basically it involves the stimulation and awakening of the functions of the right brain.

Successful self-exploration begins to integrate and connect the two hemispheres together, vitalising nervous channels for the electrical contacts to interact more positively and continuously, awakening dormant brain cells into activity. Usually these two hemispheres tend to operate in an independent manner, forming within the individual two distinct and irregularly related types of consciousness, which often leads to friction within people who lack a means to integrate two disparate tendencies. Therapy, however, can create neurological connections, which due to the relational functioning of the right brain, increase the individual's awareness of meaning, purpose and life direction.

The brain is capable of withstanding many changes, and it is widely recognised that we normally only use a small fraction of its capacity, and that we still fail to comprehend the miraculous potential that it possesses. Through the function of the brain we can give order to our experiences, we can re-sort this database, re-ordering into a variety of different world-views; we can learn how to integrate this knowledge into a holistic vision of our role in the universe, and we can transcend even our conscious knowledge and understanding through a 'leap' into the universal mind and directly experiencing a higher order of reality beyond time and space which is termed 'one-ness'.

One way of reaching these potential stages of development is through the ancient paths of meditation and withdrawal into an inner orientation. The use of biofeedback machines indicates that prolonged meditation changes the nature of the brainwaves. There are the common beta rhythms, which respond to the 'external frequencies of the outer world', and everyday life, which because of its repetitiveness and mundanity we tend to filter out anyway. These cause relatively small brainwave fluctuations, which are ignored by the individual as being relatively meaningless – just part of the everyday stress of normal experience.

The more interesting rhythms are those of the alpha and theta waves. These arise when the individual is relaxed, perhaps even sleepy, or through meditation and inner exploration. They indicate a movement towards right-brain activity, and with repetition connect those neuro-circuits and facilitate a shift into a new higher level of brain activity and organisation. These cause larger brain-wave fluctuations, which are 'expansive' in nature, and also shake older fixed patterns of behaviour apart. They agitate and can trigger transformation.

The nature of the alpha/theta waves and the right-brain association suggests that it is through these or parallel routes that the energy and vibration of the transpersonal planets is received by the individual. Conscious assimilation of the transpersonal vibration is still only made by the minority, those who have been able to attune to the whole-making patterns of the right hemisphere; other people receive them as projections of their unconscious which manifest as 'fate'. It appears then, that the transpersonal energy of Uranus, Neptune and Pluto also causes larger brainwave fluctuations, which break down rigid structural patterns within the individual and society, and eventually lead to some kind of profound change.

The interrelationship of body-brain-mind is also found in the dawning realisation that the quality and nature of the individual thoughts, attitudes and emotions can alter the balance and nature of the brain's chemistry. The brain secretes different chemicals as a response to activity in the two hemispheres, such as peptides and endorphins. The latter have several functions – including acting as an analgesic, modulating brain-cell activity, and chemically tuning or broadcasting neural sensory messages through the brain circuitry. It is probably through such routes that body functioning control by yogic mental methods is achieved, such as the slowing down of heart-rates, reduction of blood pressure, and consciously altering brainwaves by will. Current medical investigation is enquiring into the application of drugs to influence the activity and secretions of the brain; this can have future use in perhaps stimulating right-brain adjustment within an increasing number of people, who then experience a holistic perception of life, as has been experienced by many who have experimented with psychedelic drugs.

Most forms of restructuring will create a better relationship between body, brain and mind, fine-tuning the organic mechanism, and deepening the quality and quantity of information received through the senses. Much of the attraction of the psychedelic drug culture was the experience of life as multi-coloured and multi-dimensional, and that sense of connectedness which was so much more appealing than the usual experience of reality; the world had become magical, seemingly transformed through the changing of thoughts. Any real reorganisation of the body-mind will be of benefit to both polarities, as the total field of individual energy becomes vitalised and more responsive.

Re-structuring often results as a response to stress. Kapleau's book *The Three Pillars of Zen* gives several individual accounts of *satori* (the lightning flash of enlightenment-insight into the nature of things), and often the *satori* was the 'escape or culmination' of a period of inner tension and stress, caused either by self-exploration or through life events. Even in the microcosmic world of our gene structure, a parallel situation develops. Genes are also in a state of flux, where there is an element of revolution striving to create new potentialities. This evolutionary development hidden deep within our genetic structure has an ongoing process which breaks existing patterns in order to form new ones, which one assumes are designed to be more suitable for conditions of life.

Both the genetic structure and the two hemispheres of the brain have points in common, which also reflect that traditional opposition between the astrological Saturn and Uranus. As we have observed, the left brain is basically traditional and conservative, reactionary in type (Saturn) and the right brain is more radical and innovative (Uranus). But genes too appear to present similar qualities. It appears that genes have 'male or female dimensions' in that 'female genes' are resistant to alteration and conservative in essence, and maintain the status quo, whilst the 'male genes' are more pliable and accept changes and mutations quite naturally. So even in our microcosmic foundations, there is an intrinsic conflict in the gene pool which is reminiscent of the Saturn–Uranus principles.

Stress and conflict are coded into our very nature; opposition and internal friction appear as the spur to goad us into moving onwards, some willingly, some dragging their feet. But change and restructuring are inevitable, and if we resist we lose; only by co-operation can we benefit. Moving forward from our current position means progress towards the experiences of illumination and enlightenment, those visions of wholeness. It appears clear that such spiritual experiences are derived (at least in part) by the mind suddenly operating through the right-brain neuro-circuits, hence the impressions of a universe overflowing with 'meaning', and the feelings of a cohesive unity. By its very nature the left brain is incapable of offering such an experience. Yet the period following the sudden opening of the mind is concerned with the integration of the two hemispheres, so that both are active and can be accessed by the mind. Operating through either hemisphere is not the answer, linking and relating them together as a functioning unit is the real intention; we need to live through both, to relate the part to the greater context of the whole, to see the 'trees and the wood', to see our local environment as part of a global network, and ourselves as part of the one humanity. Individual evolution is inextricably linked to collective evolution. Similar to the theories of morphic resonance, the unfoldment of even a single individual into holistic consciousness makes it easier for others to follow; the new mutated pattern now exists within the collective mind and genetic structure. The Uranian revolution is only just beginning.

So, how can we participate? What can we do? Ideally, we all become enlightened, but as that is unlikely at this stage, perhaps even transforming our world-views and personal attitudes will be a great step forward. There is always plenty of personal therapy to do, new ways to look at ourselves through different approaches. Astrology itself offers such a variety of ways to generate data through a natal chart, transits, progressions, synastry, etc., that it can be hard enough just dealing with all that and with the inner archetypal factors. There are new ways to express our creativity; too much work, too little time!

As Jefferson Airplane sang some twenty years ago, 'We are the future, we are the revolution, we are the people our parents warned us against.' Holistic world-views are the key to the future, but in the process of arriving there, they will break down many of the current assumptions about life and the individual, and this will be a painful experience for society. And as the song from 'Hair' indicated, the

'Age of Aquarius' is the time of 'the mind's true liberation' . . . musicians mediating and predicting the overshadowing changes.

Modern science is now revealing that our social structures are out of phase with the nature of the universe. Increasingly we are moving away from natural harmony as a consequence of the dominating separatist world-view, and this is becoming ecologically dangerous. Dualistic consciousness needs to be seen as a fallacy, only a partial truth at best, which operates as a dangerous illusion when dominating mental attitudes and thought. New paradigm changes aim to heal these illusions of divisive opposites, providing a model that essentially duplicates the symbol of the Tao, with the interpenetrating Yin and Yang. Everything in the universe is seen as an unfolding process in action. Alternate realities are hypothesised, the universe is understood as paradoxical, and mind is increasingly perceived as creating 'material reality' through a human brain 'programme' which forms the appearance of physical reality, and then convinces us that illusion is real.

The General Systems theory (or perspectivism) is a concept of inclusiveness. This proposes that nothing should be considered in isolation, and that real understanding does not reside in fragmented analysis and separatist thinking. The part should be perceived in relation to the whole system; each system part is engaged in an ongoing interaction with all the other contributing parts, to such a degree of interdependency that cause and effect cannot be separated. Each part then reflects the result, which is both cause and effect. The main message of this is the importance of understanding the interconnected nature of reality, and that relationship is the core foundation; new scientific paradigms are exploring life as relationship, and this is the way forward. As astrologers, we attempt to apply the General Systems theory to an analysis of a natal chart, slowly building up a picture of the dynamics and inner relationships implied by all the astrological data, in order to shed a light on the whole individual. In this analogy, the 'parts' are the planets, aspects, houses, etc., and the system is the organic individual.

Similarly, humanistic and transpersonal astrologers have world-views which parallel the theories of syntropy and holism. The prefix *syn* implies relationship and connections, parts coming together; *tropy* (Greek *trope*) means transformation. Thus in syntropy parts come together and in doing so cause a reaction through which something new can happen. Part of the theory of syntropy is the idea that all living systems have an inherent impulse to perfect their total potentiality. Holism is that invisible but underlying organising principle inherent in nature, and implies integration and relationship into wholes, and the belief that evolutionary unfoldment can occur as a result of conscious self-creativity. The astrologer believes in human potentiality, expressed through inner and outer relationships, and an ongoing evolutionary progression through personally stimulated inner change (i.e. psychotherapies), and generally will advise clients through such a perspective, hopefully aiding them to become more whole.

The world of quantum physics is like an interconnected web of potentials, events, relationships, sudden changes (particle quantum leaps) and parallels the world which the astrologer explores; the web of the natal chart. Within the subatomic world, matter does not exist as a static entity, as the contradictory nature of the particle-wave shows (a particle is both a fixed point with small volume and also a wave pattern spreading over a large space); things become paradoxical and contain their opposites. With the co-existing particle wave we see 'tendencies to exist, and tendencies to occur'; astrology parallels this too, as basically we are dealing with astrological probability factors, based on the nature of the planetary energies involved, and the likelihood that certain results (tendencies/personal characteristics) will occur through those relationships. Essentially our analyses are founded upon probability factors, and because of the diversity of potential planetary relationship combinations, we have to rely upon 'tendencies to occur', intuition and speculative decisions – otherwise known as the art of astrology.

MAGICAL CREATIVE TECHNIQUES

Moving from the world of quantum physics, brain physiology, and scientific paradigms into a magical perspective may seem a large leap, yet traditional magical approaches, with their emphasis on mind exploration, can offer ways to contact other universal dimensions, and teach us how to work with the creative power of the universe.

A simple definition of magic is the art of causing changes to occur in consciousness. As the whole universe is conscious in varying ways and degrees, the scope for ourselves as individuals and fragments of this conscious life is infinite. Such changes in consciousness will be both individual and collective due to the intrinsic nature of the web of relationships, and the fact that any metamorphosis of the 'individual mind' will have a corresponding impact upon the 'collective mind', linking and transforming the polarities of both the internal and external worlds. If we change, so does the world. The revolution starts with us.

Many of the old secrets of the esoteric schools are now publicly available, as if Uranus (the ruler of the occult path) has opened most of the secret doors, enabling us to move more easily towards the 'mind's true liberation'. It is time for mankind to co-operate consciously with the creative work of the gods, and we can work with Uranus to aid in the manifestation of his futuristic dream-idea. I want to indicate a few of these techniques that can enable us to stimulate our own inner revolution and participate in a re-structuring of the world, and which parallel the original function of Uranus as the founding father who expressed the spiritual techniques that on a higher plane formed our reality. In such ways, we can begin to align ourselves with the work of the transpersonal planets, their energies and their gods.

As we have seen in the exploration of the body–brain–mind continuum, and in the look at current scientific paradigms, fixed patterns and beliefs held in the mind condition our experience of reality. If our dominating brain programming is 'fixed and closed', then much of life is denied existence or easy access into individual experience; options become restricted, freedom to change is inhibited, and the basic outlook is reactionary, and backwards-looking. If the attitudes are more fluid and open, then potential and options are maximised, more aspects or dimensions of life can be explored and experienced, the impulse to change will be more easily co-operated with, and the outlook will be revolutionary and evolutionary. Simply put, we will determine and create our future by the views we hold.

My concern is with restructuring, individually and collectively. This can occur through insight and flashes of understanding, by learning new skills, falling in love, by mystical/political/psychological conversions. Magic is a word to indicate this way, alchemy is another; the intent is the same: transformation. The traditional adult view of childhood is of a magical world of wonder, amazement and adventure, which is often viewed nostalgically as something which has been lost. Yet all that has happened is that in the process of entering the 'adult world' we have closed our minds to this perception of the universe. If we choose, it can be rediscovered; even contemporary psychotherapies often apply old magical techniques for integration and insight into the nature of the individual mind. As astrologers probing the worlds of the archetypal gods, we should reintegrate our association with magical techniques and attitudes, because in so doing, we can find an effective way to enter into a direct relationship with our planetary gods and energies.

CREATIVE VISUALISATION

This involves the power of inner imagination to change the personal life, through problem-solving and healing psychological splits. It is a form of re-programming, which is self-developed along lines suitable to personal needs. 'Imaging' assumes the theory that events are affected by what we imagine and visualise, and that in many ways we create our own future through the preoccupations of mind and emotions, which through repetitive brooding attract corresponding events or situations into our lives. Thus a restructured and re-programmed mind could attract what it needs and repulse experiences and problems that it chooses not to have.

The fundamental belief is that all is energy, and that through the use of the creative imagination, this energy will follow the direction of our focused thought, thus eventually manifesting our willed purpose. The process of creation starts as an idea or image, which when fully clarified can act as a magnetic force which affects the matter of the physical plane to conform to the creative idea. Imagination is the wielder and manipulator of the universal energies.

People who continually worry about some negative event occurring in the future are quite likely to generate situations that will make their worry come true, because energy has been externalised and in following their thought patterns will stimulate the appropriate outer reaction. They have attracted the reality that they have been worrying about. Conversely, positive projections of energy and thought-patterns can attract favourable situations, manifesting as the result of desires and needs.

Using this technique creatively can lead to personal restructuring, in which outgrown patterns and attitudes can be replaced by more suitable and positive ones. It can enable the user to move through periods of change and transition, to heal splits within the personality as indicated by antagonistic planetary placements, and offer a means of achieving an internal dialogue between the planetary archetypes. Whilst the end results of such a technique depend upon the efficacy of the individual application, it can still be useful in offering a means by which to take control of the personal life and reprogramme it in a consciously chosen way, rather than submitting passively to what seems to be an inescapable fate.

The goal can be set on any level of life; it may be to improve or affect the quality of the physical-plane life, perhaps stabilise and adjust emotions and relationships, or to develop more beneficial personal characteristics like calmness, humour, and self-discipline. The intention is clarified according to what is desired to change, a clear image or idea is focused and energised through regular remembrance (or in meditation), and it is summed up through a verbal affirmation.

For instance, someone who intends to become more creative and to unfold latent talents, could visualise themselves performing the actual form of creativity that is desired, such as painting, imagine their work on display in a gallery, and summarise this as 'I am now an open channel for artistic inspiration and creativity, and my work will be enjoyed by others.' This may take time to occur, and is dependent on a latent talent being there (and self-evaluation is a necessary first step in the technique), but such a visualisation and affirmation can help to actualise the dream, because it generates and focuses energy in a specific manner. Another affirmation could be 'I accept all my feelings as part of myself', which could be usefully employed by someone who has been denying or repressing certain emotions and feelings, as could be revealed by indications in the natal chart. A revolution can occur by such self-directed acts of re-programming. Areas such as health, life appreciation, relationships, and contacting the higher self can all be approached through this technique.

It is a tool to facilitate change, and as such could be carefully incorporated into astrological analysis, as a means to harmonise disparate energies through creating a 'bridging formula'. The summation and affirmation has a mantric quality, embodying the total intent, and is a form of autogenics (self-suggestion word hypnosis), which will also connect to the work of the 7th Ray as described in Chapter 7.

Through learning how to direct our lives through the use of mind, we can gain a key to future collaboration to build a new world structure. This is thought-form building, which is taught in several esoteric schools, but is mainly orientated towards work on the level of the collective mind.

There are several aspects to this, and the process can only be briefly indicated here. One aspect can include the cleansing of this level of the collective mind, which contains thought-forms built up by many generations of people and races, such as religious beliefs, political philosophies, racial and cultural attitudes, cumulative human desires, needs, emotions and actions. Working in this way involves the radiatory activity of light breaking down restrictive illusion-creating thought-forms, making channels available for the universal mind to be more easily contacted and to receive the impressions from that high level. Also, progressive and inclusive thought-forms are anchored there, where similar to the more personally orientated 'creative visualisation techniques', regular focusing upon them by a group can impulse the radiatory activity of the thought-form idea, so that others in the world can contact it, or be influenced in their thinking by its presence. Esotericists would believe that the contemporary scientific explorations into holism and mystical realms have been inspired by the scientific pioneers contacting such thought-forms. Occult thinking and knowledge is usually much more advanced than is recognised. This form of activity is generally considered to be 'service to the race, or world service' and is a specialist activity which trained and focused minds can participate in, and which essentially involves contributing to the manifesting divine plan as symbolised by Uranus, the idealistic visionary.

Another approach which has recently gained acceptance is that of pathworking. This has emerged through psychotherapies in the form of guided meditations and mind games, even appearing in the role-playing games like 'Dungeons and Dragons', and through the increasing public taste for fantasy in books and the cinema. In this context, however, it is the role of pathworking as doorways between the inner and outer worlds of mind that is important. Through the medium of creative imagination, it becomes possible to contact those archetypes and realms of the unconscious by an easier route, thus stimulating transformations of consciousness. Often these approaches take the form of a symbolic story and scenario, which has elements of a mythic exploration as their foundation. Usually it is a prepared storyline, which guides the individual into participating in an inner world; the symbolic creatures, characters and story are often taken from traditional sources like the Tarot, Qabalah, Greek, Egyptian and Celtic God-myths, Archetypes and Astrological planets.

For the astrologer, these techniques offer an added dimension both to his personal astrological experience, and in the tools that he can use to indicate to others how they can heal themselves and unfold their potential. Whilst chart analysis can offer a surprisingly clear picture of challenging areas, there is often a lack of supportive follow-through, of mutually developing a programme of change. Pathworking can offer the explorative astrologer a technique to enter into a more direct relationship with the planetary and mythological gods and energies, to develop their own unique inner contacts with the transformative powers, so that apart from an intellectual understanding of astrology, the astrologer becomes a living embodiment of star-lore, a transmitting channel of interpersonal energies.

We grow through integrating our divided brain and mind, awaken ourselves to a greater wholeness, perhaps through visualisation and pathworking, and due to this activity, prepare ourselves to share in the work of the great idealist, Uranus.

CHAPTER 4

Uranus and Planetary Aspects

THE NATAL ASPECTS OF URANUS need to be carefully analysed, as they hold essential information concerning the more obvious ways that Uranus will operate and reveal its activity through the natal chart. They become intrinsic patterns of personality expression, and because of their restless, stimulatory and agitatory nature, should generally be quite recognisable even if they are not personally acknowledged. It can be an interesting exercise to study your own major Uranus aspects, and see how strongly you are conditioned by their influence. A basic overview of the nature of the five major aspects may be useful at this point.

CONJUNCTION

The conjunction, or close alignment of at least two planets, is usually considered to be the most potent aspect. This involves a merging of the undiluted energies and characteristics of the planets which are in conjunction, and can be seen as a channel through which the functions of these planets can be more easily expressed via the personality. Often, these combined tendencies are asserted with considerable vigour by the individual, who may consciously recognise that they are expressions of personal power and individuality in social situations, yet this assertiveness is often achieved with a less than conscious awareness of its impact upon others.

There is an ambiguity about the influence of the conjunction, often derived from the nature of this inner tension and challenge of blending of energies which may well be uncomplementary or even antagonistic in nature. This often reveals itself through difficulties in relationships with others, especially in those situations where you may need to moderate or control your responses in order to prevent friction occurring. Such a 'lifeskill' may need to be learnt for social living, but should never be over-used so that you develop a pattern of inhibition of your thoughts and feelings when in company. What is required is sensitivity to the fact that in certain situations it may be wiser and more harmonious to remain quiet, or at least to tread carefully. Certainly this blended energy almost insists on its need to be expressed, and channels for this are consciously sought in the spheres of life indicated by the house position of the planets concerned.

The ease and efficacy with which a person can apply these energies in daily life depends to some extent on the affinity of the planets involved. They can flow almost magically together, enabling certain talents and qualities to emerge spontaneously and miraculously into effective creative channels once a focused attempt at drawing them through has been made. The right use of the personal resources is then achieved for the benefit of the individual and ideally for others too.

If the planets are lacking affinity or ease of collaboration, then utilising the energy will be more difficult, and an inner struggle is likely to create inner adjustments to enable the energies to work better with each other. A conjunction is a point of concentrated power in the natal chart if it can be properly released.

SEXTILE ASPECT (60 DEGREE ASPECT)

The sextile indicates a natural energy relationship between the planets involved, and has a particular association with the mental level. According to which planets are involved, indications are given as to the nature of the person's mind and the likely natural content of their thought-patterns. It facilitates the ability to absorb information, to collate and synthesise fragments of knowledge into a whole and to communicate this to others. It is often associated with a talent for creative expression, especially using words, and helps to build a catholic mental outlook on life built on the ability to grasp the intellectual knowledge and cultural developments of man.

There is an openness about the influence of the sextile that aids harmony, as it is not closed-minded in its inner effect, and this is conducive to the development of curiosity, space for new/other perceptions, and an ease in the wider social environment and in group co-operation.

TRINE ASPECT (120 DEGREE ASPECT)

The trine is a positive reconciliatory aspect, capable of uniting in a working manner two apparently opposing energies; hence its symbol being like a triangle. A trine can be used to resolve areas of difficulty associated with any hard or challenging aspects which are made to either of the planets involved. As the symbol of the triangle is associated with understanding and resolving dualism, the trine aspects involving Uranus and any other planet are likely to hold a key to processes of personal integration, healing and transformation, and should be carefully considered in this light.

SQUARE ASPECT (90 DEGREE ASPECT)

The square aspect between planets indicates an energy relationship of tension and challenge which cannot be resolved without some form of internal adaptation being achieved. Potentially, the results of working with the square can lead to greater inner harmony, but this is likely to occur only after prolonged effort and psychological frustration. Through such refining fires the character becomes reborn in some essential way. It often seems to indicate barriers in the individual psyche, which repeatedly block a chosen route.

There are 'lessons and challenges' that the square represents that cannot be avoided, inevitable crises that will require confronting as stages along the path of life. Squares are frustrating, a source of inner conflict which unless the nettle of challenge is grasped, will have a negative effect upon the life and thwart many a desire and intention. If the square is 'overcome', then it serves as a point of release for power and energy which can be applied to achieve personal aims. The square is associated with internal psychological problem areas, and an attempt to restructure the inner life, mind or emotions is vitally necessary.

OPPOSITION ASPECT (180 DEGREE ASPECT)

The opposition is often more concerned with the outer objective world and with relationships with others, but unless the personal focus is entirely orientated towards achievement in the outer world it is likely to prove less of a constant personal struggle than the inner square. Whereas the square represents a unique, private, personal challenge, the opposition tends to be projected outwards (similar to the Shadow) onto others, thus creating a context in which the conflict can be realised, observed and worked with. There can be signs of compulsive behaviour, demands made upon others, expressions of the power of focused will and self-absorption which often have an interfering effect within close relationships, coupled with attempts to manipulate others for personal gain.

Creative and harmonious relationships can help to resolve the conflict between the opposition of planetary energies; also, any trines or sextiles to either opposition planet can help to resolve the problems.

URANUS ASPECTS

Aspects made by Uranus to any natal planet are significant in revealing an area of life where there is a need for expansion and freedom. These aspects are like an unlocked door onto new horizons; the individual need only turn the handle.

Irrespective of the nature of the aspect, it represents a potential which can be grasped either through an easy application of mutually harmonious planetary energies, or through an inner struggle to transmute the more challenging aspects in to their more positive dimension.

These doors to the 'new' are where the individual can widen his life experiences, become aware of new perceptions and insights, be free to experiment and become excited by the new stimulation of feeling liberated from older restrictive patterns of behaviour and lifestyle. Then there is more freedom to release and express that individuality which has been imprisoned, to cast away – if necessary – those social behavioural imprints that have been imposed as a process of social education and which reflect the dominant social ethos. This can involve the re-creation of the self where the theme of creativity becomes the main operative principle.

Often, society has an ambiguous attitude towards creativity. In theory it is supportive, valuing its role in cultural development; yet the individual associated with creativity and free expression is often frowned on as being socially subversive. For potentially creative individuals, there is the ongoing social and economic pressure to conform and take the socially acceptable paths through life. Collectively, there is always a feeling of unease and possible threat when we are confronted by someone who chooses an unconventional personal appearance, or who has an obviously nonconformist personal philosophy. Such people, who have chosen to be more personally creative (if only through a choice of clothes or hairstyles) have at least taken a step away from unconscious conformism to feel some sense of uniqueness. Creativity can manifest in the work to build a suitable lifestyle that actually fits the person, rather than just falling into the social trap of 'the way we should be'. Re-creating oneself is a difficult but valuable process, which demands that one stands apart from mainstream society to gain a clearer perspective. This is creativity just as much as literary or artistic expressions are. Creativity is always potentially subversive, as it can offer new perceptions, insights, ways of living, and as such can shake the traditions and static ways of society. Uranian creativity is likely to reflect this need to re-create self through nonconformity.

The quality of the Uranus vibration is often one of friction, which appears to be released into the psyche at an irregular frequency and rhythm. Because it is highly charged, fluctuating and expressing positive and negative characteristics simultaneously, its spasmodic impact upon the nervous system can cause stress and tension. Life suddenly feels speeded up and energised, changes can begin to occur with rapidity, and a feeling that things are running away from conscious control is likely, with new insights into life and self flooding the mind, and bursts of creative activity or business ideas happening.

It is an electrifying phase, and it will take some time to assimilate and integrate the new directions that are intuitively felt to be necessary. For someone who has been strongly identified with personality structures, and who is dependent upon them for security in life, this can be a very difficult phase to endure. Feelings of bewilderment are common which may also trigger psychosomatic nervous illnesses or breakdowns as the inner foundations are shaken apart.

Alternatively, for someone capable of riding the crests of these waves of change like a surfer, these phases can prove to be highly liberating and represent turning-points in their lives which enable them to live more freely and in tune with themselves. In such a case, it can give that needed boost to the energy with which they free themselves from a limiting environment – inner or outer – and so re-create their life through freeing energy to actualise their dreams.

SUN–URANUS CONJUNCTION

With this aspect, you are likely to experience ongoing clashes and discord with others and society. This is due to the fact that your essential tendency is to be highly individualistic and nonconformist, and that this will inevitably bring you into conflict with the traditions and social lifestyle patterns.

You will not have a passive nature, or acquiesce easily in what is required of you by parents, school, religion or the state; but you will be a passionate, rebellious spirit rejecting, questioning or opposing those pressures which you either disagree with or believe are intended to inhibit your freedom.

This 'passion', however, is not really emotionally rooted, but is your way of releasing a build-up of energy within your nature which has to find some means of release, similar to the boiling of water which transforms into steam to escape from a container. The slightest threat or fear of 'imprisonment' and you will begin looking for the escape route.

This need for freedom – in whichever and however many ways you personally define 'freedom' – will be a dominant factor influencing your life. This energy's urgent need for expression will have an unsettling impact upon your adult choices and life direction. As a result of experiencing this inner pressure for change, you are likely to observe the elements of unpredictability flowing into your established life patterns, like the steam escaping from the boiling water. In some ways this could be good and beneficial, but an energy acting in uncontrolled unconscious ways can severely disrupt a relatively harmonious individual or family lifestyle, just because someone under its influence begins to act in a potentially destructive manner. Just 'throwing the energy away', attempting to reduce the inner pressure, is not constructive or sensible. This inner process indicates that change is needed, and this will usually be associated with a particular sphere of life, as indicated by the house through which Uranus is transiting. Conscious attention is required to tune into the messages being triggered internally so that the energy can be directed into suitable channels of expression.

You will have to acknowledge and confront the implications of that innate hatred of restrictions that life invariably imposes through family, employment and society. You will struggle against them all of your life, wanting to be 'free', but free to do what? And free to live in what way, and where? Probably you will lack real answers, but a search to find a satisfying direction is crucial for you, otherwise in gaining your freedom you will discover that through cutting the ties you have become personally lost, or have destroyed those foundations that you only now recognise are important and meaningful for you.

In your intimate relationships, you will have to be aware of your tendency to invest your own needs with supreme value and importance, to insist upon your own individual rights and freedom to express your own nature without compromising, yet often failing to offer the same to your partner. You can have a problem with impatience tinged with intolerance, which can create friction, as can your attraction towards areas of experience that some consider to be unorthodox or deviant. Not that such reactions unduly concern you; in fact you may feel tempted to flaunt any such preferences in front of others.

Probably you will be attracted towards entering sudden intense and exciting physical and emotional relationships, especially those spontaneous ones that can occur without too much awareness of any future implications. You prefer 'newness', through exploring the unknown and devising different variations and may often shy away from commitment and responsibility, partly from fear and partly from an inability to consider your partner's needs as highly as your own. The problem is how to balance your need for new experiences, and your hatred of restriction, and your desire for absolute personal freedom, with the demands of living with people in society.

You need to become more mature in relationships, to become more aware of the value of mutual sharing, to care as much for your partner as you do yourself, and by helping them to express the totality of their own nature and not inhibiting their personal development by the dominating insistence of your needs. Learn to walk side by side into freedom and fulfilment.

Recognising these tendencies in your nature is the first step to begin taking conscious control and use of the energies, so that your life begins to work better, becomes more meaningful and satisfying.

One such direction that you may find helps in this self-renewal, reorientation and personal exploitation lies in expressing your urge for exploration, of investigating new horizons and interests; but try not to live this out in a purely self-centred way, but also through relationships.

Quite naturally, your mind is attuned to the Uranian 'higher mind' or 'Universal Mind'. This implies that there is an innate power there, and that your mind is capable of taking sudden leaps and making connections which can offer new insights or ways of looking at life. Whilst in many this can be too erratic and undisciplined to be utilised fully, the natural direction in which it moves is futuristic. This is a reaction against the restrictions of established patterns and predictable, static social traditions – the revolutionary spirit – and is also a tool to be used in the visualisation and formation of possible future societies. Combining your natural tendency towards permissiveness and your need for creative expression, you may explore and develop yourself in terms of progressive futuristic philosophies and attitudes, associating with like-minded groups and individuals, to help build the Aquarian New Humanity. Embodying new lifestyle patterns and more open attitudes can offer a new world for you to explore now and one which can benefit others too. Here lies freedom without current restriction, together with the opportunity to express your rebellious nature in the face of social limitations. Hopefully, you will help to build a more understanding and free world for everyone to share, as you transform your initial self-preoccupation into concern for the group, where self-benefit will benefit all.

Sun–Uranus Sextile

The radical energies of Uranus are potentially more easily expressed in both the sextile and the trine than in the conjunction. Whereas an important shift may need to occur in the individual with the conjunction aspect – in order to renew and redirect his overflowing insistent Uranian energy – these other two dynamic harmonious aspects are ripe for exploitation and personal unfoldment.

You should have a naturally progressive outlook, and a sense of affinity with society which is directed towards affirming its positive side and its potential for improvement and life-enhancement for others. The assertive and possibly aggressive rebellious stance is already transformed within you into a reformist tendency. 'Change from within' is your keynote, rather than a direct destructive attack or a negative opting out of society.

Your mind will be very active, searching, questioning, and naturally explorative, and will have a need for creative self-expression. It will be important to you to be individual and personally assertive, but undue eccentricity is not your style. You will feel more of a 'centre' to your being than will the individual with the conjunction, a more stable inner character and ability to direct your life and make wise choices. Tolerance and understanding of others will be more evident, especially an intellectually derived tolerance based on your innate humanitarian instincts, although often your emotional affinity with others can be a little cold or withdrawn. You do not feel yourself at one with the world, yet intellectually your mind is; perhaps more empathy is required.

You are likely to ally yourself with those groups which support futuristic reforming tendencies, and have the attitude to 'change the world to be a better place for everyone to live in'. Probably you could rise to positions of importance in such groups, becoming a spokesperson for their visions and ideals, transmitting your enthusiasm and positivity through those channels. Your opinions are usually forthright, and you try to stay true to them and be committed to your beliefs. Honesty and openness are high on your list of essential values, and you have little tolerance for lies and deceits and those who perpetrate them; this can easily lead you towards opposing national governments or establishment groups who are 'economical with the truth' on orders from their 'superiors'. Equally, it could lead you to break away from groups that you are associated with if they – in your opinion – fall to such levels or compromise and fail to live up to the high ideals which they may offer to the public.

You believe that life has an inner meaning of great value, and continually search for the threads of this in all of your life experience, trusting in the belief that life is good, often despite appearances. However, you are aware of the darker sides of existence, and feel inspired to try to improve the quality of life for those who suffer or for generations to come.

At times, especially perhaps after any disappointments on your path, you may coolly withdraw from relationships or social involvement. See this only as a temporary phase for re-evaluation. You need like minds, and should continue to communicate with them, sharing experiences, insight and knowledge. This may easily develop over time into forms of teaching where through sharing you can contribute towards progress for others, and this could become a fulfilling route for you to follow.

SUN–URANUS TRINE

As with the sextile, the energy emanating from the trine aspect is harmonious in nature and can be positively assimilated. Most of the characteristics of the sextile are repeated with the trine.

The natural attunement with the 'Universal Mind' should help you to receive valid insights and intuitions, especially at times when the trine is activated by transit or progression movements, which offer opportunities for enhanced creativity and useable ideas.

The futuristic tendencies will obviously be present, but it is likely that with the trine, such ideas are founded on a more immediately practical basis, possibly as a result of an attitude which is more rooted in a scientific, rational perspective.

You should find it relatively easy to exploit your natural creativity, as this aspect releases a large quantity of potentially productive ideas into those areas of life in which you need inspiration. Aided by the ability to persevere and apply a focused will, you should have no real obstacles confronting you in your efforts to manifest your creative ideas. These can take a myriad of forms, through experimentation, innovation, or modification of existing products.

There is likely to be an inner sense of detachment in your searches and creativity, a perpetual fascination with inquiry, coupled with a creativity which works through the creator, and is never perceived egotistically. This can help you to become quite productive in your chosen sphere, and also quite varied too, as you look around to find suitable ways in which to stretch your wings and explore new horizons.

Your reformist, idealistic and humanitarian tendencies can find success through communication and sharing with others, and this can be important to your sense of well-being, as you do need to feel that you are of some use to others. Your sense of commitment, enthusiasm and positivity can be most helpful in supporting others, or through transmitting these energies to help motivate group endeavours. Your personal relationships can also benefit from this outpouring of optimism and positivity and sense of mutual sharing.

SUN–URANUS SQUARE

The square has several characteristics to the opposition, but the frustrated energy of the square can turn towards a more aggressive and potentially violent form of expression if there is no suitable channel for it to be released into. The need to discover adequate forms into which the Uranian energy can be successfully anchored is common to all these aspects made to natal Uranus, and is a perpetual Uranian task.

Inwardly, you will be erratic, individualistic, restless and nervously agitated, desiring independence and freedom from all social restrictions. You are a natural dissenter, a social troublemaker, preferring to support a minority view of one; it is even likely that in radical groups your tendency to dissent will lead to becoming isolated and alienated from those who are in basic agreement with you. If unmodified, this energy indiscriminately released is quite capable of 'causing trouble in an empty house'! Being the devil's advocate is a function that can often lead to personal confusion and loss of self, as eventually you either erode or lose sight of your own personal attitudes, beliefs or ideals that you initially held. To you, if the majority hold a certain opinion or belief then that

fact alone requires you to reject it. From a more inclusive perspective there can be some validity in such a standpoint. As Spike Milligan once said, 'Fifty million flies can't be wrong . . . so eat more dung!'

It must be remembered that such an attitude is really the intrinsic tone of the Uranian energy, but taken to a more destructive extreme. The exaltation of the unique individuality has to be achieved in a correct and wise manner, otherwise the negative destructive tendency emerges into action.

You will be undisciplined, hating predictable routines of life and work, finding it hard to act responsibly and with commitment. You react against conforming to social rules, as you feel that they inhibit your desire to be free, and you often follow your choices irrespective of the repercussions and costs of doing so.

You will probably fail to listen to well-meaning advice, and stubbornness and need for self-assertion will lead you towards those very life experiences and problems that you were being warned against. Over time, if you look honestly at your life, you will observe those times where you misjudged, made foolish decisions and choices often through sheer contrariness and the assertion of your 'free individuality'. Without awareness we are never free, but are merely prisoners of our own unconscious tendencies choosing for us, like playthings of the inner gods.

At times you may become a little paranoid, especially when your choices have been unwise. It doesn't have to be like that. You can choose to take a more conscious role in your life, and not be a victim of your own ignorance. Those 'enemies' that you like to project out there, are often your own unresolved inner demons slowly consuming you from within.

It is an aspect of frustrated, blocked transformation and renewal; the inner personal revolution that Uranus would like to bring is being inhibited. These inner tensions can become potentially violent, but need to be redirected into constructive positive channels. You may need to release these tendencies towards impracticality, antisocial attitudes and hidden urges for personal power, and use them to renew your own life; to stop being antagonistic purely for the sake of performing the adversarial role. Compromise and balancing within your own nature, and allowing an inner transformation is the key to a more satisfying relationship with the greater community, and for you to enter into more personally beneficial and harmonious intimate relationships.

As you probably recognise, you like others to be submissive to you, yet you tend to lose respect for their individuality when they are. You need to learn how to unfold and elevate their uniqueness because that is the corollary of your own personal philosophy. Emotional depths need to be stirred more, letting those poisons of frustration and emotional conflict rise to the surface to be encountered, seen and understood, released and transmuted by an acceptance of them as a shadow part of yourself which should be acknowledged and never denied. Doing so will harmonise your energies more, offer greater inner peace and tranquility (as far as Uranus will allow!), and free those festering poisons out of you. The real point of all this is to enable your uniqueness and individuality to flower in freedom, so that your life will be less about acting as a frustrated opponent, and become more what you really are and what you truly stand for, moving away from a negative expression into one of positivity. Your choice is to do this, and the benefits will be yours to enjoy.

Sun–Uranus Opposition

Both the opposition and square have several characteristics in common with the more difficult tendencies of the conjunction. These are amplified by the fact that these challenging aspects have a peculiar quality which is similar to an 'on-off switch' energy flow pattern.

Internal and external erratic behaviour is to be expected, which can lead to those dramatic and often drastic changes of behaviour and lifestyles which often affect those with the conjunction aspect.

Within your hidden inner life, you are likely to feel an undercurrent of restless activity which, whilst peaking and troughing, is always present in your life.

This can lead to nervous tensions and irritability, an edgy tone to your energy which is often psychically communicated or received by others and experienced as an intangible sense of unease. Your moods are erratic, unpredicatable and temperamental, creating sudden confusing changes in your attitudes and relationships, even to contradicting statements that you may have just made. Sometimes you may even be unaware of this lack of continuity.

There will be an emphasis upon individuality and independence, with an urge for freedom from all restrictions and an insistence upon your own needs. In some cases, this can manifest as a compulsion to display a rebellious, antisocial attitude, mainly as a reactionary explosion of energy rather than a considered response which could also offer viable alternatives. Your reactions are likely to be more negative in quality and content, and may need a conscious degree of self-moderation to avoid a traditional and instinctive 'knee-jerk' reaction. You may find that you obtain pleasure from seeing others react to your anti-establishment/traditions baiting, as it can add some excitement to life, but it is unlikely to be an inherently creative or positive action as you often fail to have anything of value which could replace whatever it is you are opposing.

In many ways you are insecure, feeling lost and frustrated with both the world and yourself. Your inner energy flow is uneven; sometimes you are highly charged and have difficulties dealing with that, other times the energy seems to be switched off, and life goes flat and colourless. You probably lack a stable cohesive centre, and you may need to struggle towards establishing a secure point of balance within your identity.

You can be hypersensitive, but tend to deny this aspect of yourself as you feel uncomfortable with your emotional nature and its tidal ebbs and flows, and it doesn't fit into that intellectualised self-image that you have developed of yourself. This can be quite delusory, but is also a prop for you to attempt to centre your identity around. These images can include considering yourself 'before your time', an unrecognised genius or artist, a cultural bohemian, a radical revolutionary, an important social adversary. Glamorous images emerge from that high opinion of yourself and those peculiar insights and ideas that you attempt to communicate to others. Indeed, there are likely to be some nuggets of gold scattered around in there, but more often than not you fail to deliver, wisps of intentions dematerialising into the air. Your evaluations of things are often impractical, and due either to distraction by newer, more glamorous ideas, or through failing to apply a disciplined will, you often fail to develop your natural gifts to the full.

Whilst you tend to insist that your will is paramount, you really need to learn effective forms of social compromise, and to realise that you are not the all-important centre of the universe which you often mistake yourself to be. Just learning to listen to other points of view and perceptions of life can teach you much. This may not come easily to you, however, as you tend to see such contact and communication as a form of challenge, pitting yourself in your mind against other points of view.

You may need to stop tilting against windmills. Not that the windmills are not there – they are, but as an effort to redirect and rediscipline your nature and energies. A redefinition of the 'revolutionary spirit' needs to be made by you, a re-channelling of your scattered energies.

Learning forms of relaxation or meditative techniques could become very important to your well-being. Highly strung, nervous states are not beneficial to health. Relationships can also be fraught with problems, as your erratic hot and cold contributions do not always fit in with your partner's behaviour patterns. You may need to be wary of making excessive emotional demands, especially as you are not balanced in your emotional nature, and probably have a lack of understanding of that level. In many ways, it is likely to be an immature aspect of your nature, and may require conscious development and exploration.

Attempts to restrict the freedom of others should also be guarded against, as should undue attractions towards promiscuity, unless you are personally liberated from any emotional reactions against such freedoms which could be also expressed by your partners.

MOON–URANUS CONJUNCTION

All Moon–Uranus aspects have an inherent conflict hidden within their effects on the personality; this is the clash between the old, established foundations and patterns as represented by the Moon, and the forward-looking, stimulatory disruptiveness of Uranus. Whilst this conflict can express its presence across every level of being, an extra dimension of the energy interrelationship lies in the Moon's affinity to the emotions and feeling, and the Uranian affinity to a more impersonal, abstract intellectualism, to the mind. This can create an inner friction between 'head and heart', which some can find to be difficult to resolve.

Emotionally, you are liable to experience regular swings of mood and an erratic, changeable feeling nature, which can make you appear to be unpredictable, unreliable, impulsive and lacking in commitment and a sense of responsibility. The Moon energies alone are fluctuating, ebbing and flowing, and conjoining these with the Uranus vibration is not conducive to a stable, controllable inner life. You will find that your inner bias will move between the extremes of Moon dominant to Uranus dominant, and only occasionally will you come to rest at a point of balance and harmony between the two. However, this point where 'head and heart' are in accord is the ideal, and in any personal development work should be the point to be aimed towards.

You will look for the unusual and the exciting in every sphere of life. Strangeness and novelty will intrigue and attract you, and this is likely to be a paramount factor in your intimate relationships. Your Moon will demand powerful, intense emotions as 'food', and Uranus will expect fascination and excitement to bewitch the mind. The problem is finding them both co-existing within one partner, and remaining there, or before long you will be looking around for someone new. Your relationships are likely to be varied and potentially cosmopolitan, ranging across a wide variety of personality types, and you may find it very difficult to determine what is the most suitable for you, and which you can benefit from in the longer term. You are often attracted to those who are really unsuitable for you, or those who pose some sort of challenge, which you find adds extra stimulation.

Much depends upon how you succeed in 'balancing' that inherent conflict between the urge for security and foundations and the urge for novelty and free experimentation. The Moon could dominate, thus imposing inner restrictions upon you, inhibiting those desires for new experiences and freedom, and creating the frustration of unlived dreams; or Uranus could pull you towards excess, where you lose your roots and stability in a total pursuit of the new and unexplored experiences irrespective of personal costs.

Socially, your life could be rich with interest and acquaintances, where your direct open style of expression coupled with intellectual analysis, realism, personal tolerance and understanding can find many who find your company stimulating and rewarding. As you often tend to reflect both sides of an issue – evading a commitment to choose sides and become partisan – you can act as a diplomatic foil between adversaries, as well as being able to retain the friendship and contact.

It may be that you will eventually prefer to live an independent life, where you choose not to restrict yourself to any one partner, but aim to have personal freedom to change as you will. This can result from an inability to stay committed and interested in a traditional relationship; or through problems partly created by your emotional flexibility and moods where in the midst of confusion, you still insist upon your right to be self-determining, even if you have no clear idea of what it is you want at that time.

Moon–Uranus Sextile

Both the sextile and trine aspects confer an easier inner response to the Moon–Uranus energy relationship. There is a fluency to the energy flow and merger that offers considerable potential to those with these aspects.

You should find that there is less reliance upon the past and established patterns of lifestyle and behaviour, certainly less sense of conflict or confusion whenever you are responding to the future orientation of Uranus. Also your 'head and heart' will be beating more as one rather than to different rhythms, so your relationships should be easier and more successful, and your ability to be decisive should be enhanced.

You will be mentally alert, aware when opportunities come your way, and usually ready to take the fullest possible advantage of them. You are prepared to take risks and speculative leaps in order to capitalise upon an idea or venture. Learning will come easily to you, and you will learn quickly from experience. You have the ability to pour an enthusiastic energy into all of your projects to increase their likelihood of success. Signs of this should have been evident in your childhood; you probably developed and matured earlier than the majority. A feeling of independence and unique-ness is likely to have arisen in you, which can create a stable centre to work from and be a source of energy for you to exploit.

Socially, you will get on well with others, experiencing a form of empathic rapport with people, helping you to become tolerant and understanding. You may enjoy personal contact, and be attracted to expanding this into avenues of teaching or communication, where you can transmit your enthusiasms and love of exploration and discovery to others.

Your intimate relationships should be less fraught with emo-tionally triggered moods and tensions, and this will help you to succeed with more committed partnerships if you so choose. You will still be attracted to the Uranian impulses for change, variety and novelty, but the impact of that vibration will be less compulsive and demanding. If you wish, you can follow it, but can also control it too. You will need a distinct intellectual dimension in your closer relationships though, and that should be a factor in your choices. It is also likely that your life will be heavily influenced by women, and they will be important conveyers of 'destiny' for you.

Moon–Uranus Trine

The trine is similar to the sextile, but probably allows you to develop the use of this energy in a wider social context. Mentally, you will be curious, always eager to learn, finding comprehension easy, and having an ability to make use of your storehouse of information, skills and techniques that you continue to acquire throughout life. Combined with a creative imagination, you should be able to utilise this towards building new enterprises and busi-nesses, and you will have adequate energy and enthusiasm to do so, plus that essential commitment to succeed.

Your innate attraction to the new is likely to be less concerned with self-interest than with the interests of the group, and you will have an innovative attitude and perspective. Here the Uranian influence will be shining through more strongly.

Your domestic and personal life may be unconventional and unusual to some, although probably perfectly natural to yourself.

Tradition and predictable patterns of behaviour are seen as life-destroyers, limiters of freedom and exploration; and whilst you may not feel totally committed to open opposition, you certainly will not feel that you are under any obligation to give traditions more power by submitting to them if you do not choose to. Some kinds of authority you can respect, but your attitudes will be rebellious and scathing in your denunciation of misuses when you believe that abuses of power are occurring.

Using this energy will depend upon you discovering suitable channels of expression. You may need to create these yourself, or could ally with others in a communal future-orientated venture. This sense or intuition of interrelatedness acts as a guide for you, and is a very important foundational pattern in your life. Following its light should lead to the most suitable type of experiences for your development, and will satisfy that need within you to build the future now within the present.

Moon–Uranus Square

The characteristics of the square are quite similar to the opposition, reflecting that basic clash of disparate energies and levels. Relationships will be a likely battleground, and your domestic life will be unsettled as you struggle with your unresolved inner conflicts.

Whilst you are mentally alert and quite clever, one problem could be related to how you apply your talents. Finding a satisfactory outlet for them could also lead to benefits in your own inner balancing. Failure to do so, through lack of discipline and application, will only serve to amplify your inner conflicts.

You will be capable of releasing the restrictions of the past, but an ideal for you would be founded in known, established ways (the influence of the Moon), while being able to explore new horizons simultaneously (to satisfy Uranus). The problem is how to achieve this balancing act. Your usual experience involves the relinquishing of the past, so that you feel you can experience the new as freely as possible. This reflects the current world challenge of integrating the old Piscean and the new Aquarian impulse, in a way that does not necessitate widespread pain and destruction. If you can help by integrating the magnetic attractions of both the old and the new within yourself, it will be a very worthwhile contribution to society.

If you allow the Uranian impulse to dominate you, then it is likely to sweep away most of your foundations in life. Whilst this can create a temporary thrill of excitement at the potentials opening up for you, and the promise of unrestrained liberty, there will inevitably come the time when a phase of consolidation and anchoring is necessary. Unlimited freedom is hard for most to handle without losing their stability.

Within your relationships, there are several vital lessons to be learned. These are those of co-operation, commitment, responsibility, compromise and shared decision-making. You cannot expect to dominate at all times, demanding that your partner acquiesce to your will, or to bow to your need for freedom when you allow them little for themselves. Changes in your behaviour patterns to the more positive creative qualities will work wonders, and your relationships will become much more fulfilling for all concerned. Instead of rejecting your contemporary life as unsatisfying, and being willing to 'throw it away' in search of new excitements, the key to working with the Moon–Uranus energy lies in the search to transform the existing life. Ask yourself which areas you wish to change in your life. Evaluate carefully your needs, dreams and desires, and see if by transforming your current established life you would be able to satisfy most of them, without destroying existing foundations. Consider how you could change aspects of your life to create space for new interests to emerge, or what attitudes could be changed so that life became renewed, or how you could improve your relationships. Most people fail to take advantage of their potential in life, or refuse to transform themselves and their environment in order to create a more enjoyable life. It is an individual choice, but for those who, like yourself, have a rebellious streak, that energy can be use positively to change whatever is not suitable. An active not passive approach is required.

Moon–Uranus Opposition

The challenges which this opposition is likely to create will probably be focused on the sphere of your more intimate relationships. These will reflect the more direct clash between the old and the new, these known familiar patterns and the urge for a revitalising stimulation from the unknown. Your inner life may often seem to be a battleground, as the dominating energies struggle to control your choices and expression, and you are likely to feel almost torn apart at certain times of crisis.

There will be an underlying tendency towards mental and emotionally based stress, emerging from this emotional instability and the problems created within relationships through exhibiting unpredictable yet frequent changes of mood. The impact of the Uranian vibration creating sudden changes in the erratic mutability of the Moon's emotional affinity can stir already choppy seas into more dangerous storms. If you then choose to release this tension on those who are closest to you – which is a common pattern of behaviour – then your relationships could become quite stormy. The inability of others to feel themselves able to depend on you will obviously affect the building of long-term relationships.

Your need for variety and newness can also cause problems. This can be internally, in that you easily get bored and lose interest in your home, employment, marriage, lovers, etc., and then enter a phase of frustration as your need for stimulation is denied. To break out of this tension, you may suddenly 'explode' towards new explorations, attempting to shatter all limitations and restrictions. This can lead to moving house, changing employment or established careers to move in other directions, to entering affairs, or separating from marriage partners. You find responsibility and commitments hard to bear during such phases when the Uranian impulse is too strong and capable of breaking through the Moon's established defensive patterns.

What should be avoided is the repressive inner build-up of these tensions, because if they 'explode' through you then their destructive quality will dominate, rather than their transformative intent. The first step lies in acknowledging this pressure within you, and then learning to release it slowly and with conscious control into suitable channels as a natural development of your life. If you accept this impulse for new experiences and interests, it can be adequately handled, in socially acceptable ways. There then develops a continuous element of exploration in your life (especially intellectually). This is an essential safety valve to develop for your inner adjustment and well-being.

Understanding this aspect of your nature will help you in choosing a suitable partner, one who accepts this inner need of yours, and is capable and willing to compromise when necessary in helping you to find ways of safely releasing the tensions. Any progress that you can make towards integrating your emotional and mental levels together into a functioning whole will reap considerable dividends. Forms of psychotherapy devoted to personal wholeness could be explored, offering potential for positive development. Attempts by you to impose either an emotional decision or a more rational one will lead to inner friction.

The sense of instability that you often live with also reflects upon your sense of personal identity, and the result is inner insecurity. You lack a solid centre, fluctuating between the Moon and Uranus, between emotion and logic, finding a home nowhere. You could find it helpful to allow yourself to experience your emotions as fully as possible. Let them rise to the surface, feeling and understanding their intensity, without cutting them off intellectually when they become unpleasant, or dismissing them as being somehow inferior and not part of your self-image. Equally, your mental interests and pursuits should ideally have an emotionally resonant dimension to them, helping the levels to draw together. As your nervous system is overamplified, attempts like these can help to moderate and balance the flow of conjoined energies, thus making it easier for you to live with others without so frequently feeling this restless obsession with change.

MERCURY–URANUS CONJUNCTION

With the harmonious aspects, Uranus tends to work well with Mercury, as both are associated with the mind and intellect, and it is upon that level that their influence and qualities are displayed.

You are likely to have an alert, clever mind which finds great enrichment in pursuing any aspect of human life and knowledge that you are curious about. You are probably articulate and literate too. You have a natural questioning and searching attitude, always looking to increase your personal storehouse of knowledge, and attempting to derive a sense of connectedness synthesising that information into more holistic patterns.

Your immediate response to the world is one of mental exploration, rather than emotional feeling reaction. The world is perceived as an inextinguishable source of fascination, overflowing with a myriad of stimulating facts, theories and beliefs. New horizons beckon, and there seems to be scope to investigate the unusual and the different ways of living on this multi-hued planet. With so much to delve into, so many different paths that you can walk, the problem is that of choice. Where do you start? There is the fear that by choosing Route 1, you could then miss that fascinating experience down Route 66. This could be one of your weaknesses – that you lack the discipline of perseverance, and that your mind may like to flit from one intriguing subject to another that suddenly attracts your attention. Inner continuity may need to be developed, both to improve your ability to concentrate, and to make the best use of your talent for acquiring knowledge. One challenge could be in the question of how you apply your knowledge in daily life. Or is it just stored on that mental level, unconnected to real living?

You have little patience with ignorance, your own or that of anyone else. You have a compulsion to find out, and will feel restless until you have made some progress. Your mind will store those themes as 'little fascinations', subjects that have picqued your curiosity, and eventually you will have to take steps to satisfy it. You can be a little intolerant with others who have less exploratory minds, and with those who are evasive and deceitful in their interpersonal relationships. Certainly you will be best suited to a partner who can complement your searches, and who can stimulate your mind, because for you, that is the essential level of contact. Friendships will develop with others who have affinity interests, and over time you are likely to develop a wide variety of acquaintances as your interests and areas of exploration expand. Unfortunately though, you may find that you also drop older contacts due to your fascination with treading new paths, and thus losing interest in old spheres of enquiry.

You have a preference for looking towards the future, optimistic about new discoveries, even if you are studying past history. You may need to balance an emphasis towards preferring fact and a more scientific rational approach, with the more intuitive interpretative approaches to life, between the objective and the subjective styles of analysis. The influence of Mercury will be biased towards the former, whereas Uranus will tip towards a more universal, intuitive attitude of inner knowing. It is not what you know, but how you use it in life which is the key.

MERCURY–URANUS SEXTILE

Both the sextile and the trine reflect and continue the themes associated with the conjunction. There is the fluency of an alert intellectual mind, with a dexterity in using both the spoken and the written word which displays your breadth of knowledge, although sometimes you may have to be wary of a glittering superficiality with no real depth to your expression.

As you find knowledge exciting and stimulating, you like to share it with others too. This can lead towards careers where you become a communicator or teacher in some context. As you can develop a genuine understanding of what you study, this can become a viable way of helping others to learn the joys of exploration for themselves. You should ensure that you avoid becoming tied to any form of work which will restrict your mental freedom; such confinement would seem like a prison to you, and your inner tension and frustration would increase, probably having a negative effect upon your health and temper.

Freedom is essential to you; it is life-giving and health-giving to be free within your mind. It is less essential for you to feel free on either the physical or emotional levels, providing that the mind can soar. As your mind will be in a state of 'perpetual motion', you will have to learn how to relax more, find ways of releasing any build-up of inner pressure. Meditation could be a good way of doing this, especially those forms which 'enter the silence', through calming and emptying the mind. Active meditations will only agitate and stimulate you more, but a passive sitting will serve to cleanse and show you how your mind is actually working. The early days of such personal exploration could be difficult for you, but the gradual emerging of a still, calm centre could prove to be of inestimable value in your life, as well as reducing the chances of eventual nervous system problems.

To express yourself fully, you may need to learn a more disciplined approach to ensuring that you complete your chosen projects. There is always the temptation to run after some new, bright object of fascination, forgetting your partially completed plan, and thus never really achieving your objectives. Your life could be a scattering of unrealised schemes; if so, it could be wiser to tidy them up, clarify your objectives, plan a sequential scheme to manifest them, and follow your intention through to completion. Whilst you often hate to look back, there can be unfinished business there that deserves to be resolved. Even progressive thinkers need to build on the foundations laid in the past, and if those foundations are badly laid, then no future structure can ever be safely built.

MERCURY–URANUS TRINE

The trine aspect tends to add the qualities of creativity and intuition more easily to the characteristics of the conjunction and the sextile. There is a subtle shift from the urge to acquire knowledge as a predominant tendency, to one of being capable of utilising it for the benefit of self and others.

You apply your mind to establishing a firm foundation for future work, where your investigative and research interests are directed towards a clear aim and purpose. Your basic orientation is humanitarian; you prefer to put your talents and energy into spheres that you believe will make a positive contribution to human progress. This could include scientific or medical work, or knowledge communication. You see that the point of knowledge is not just to acquire it, but to use it to improve the quality of life; your inner fascination has a more practical dimension.

There is likely to be an interest in the mysteries of life, and in universal and human behaviour, and a sense of the subtle, intangible energies that animate life. This can develop into exploring the occult realms, and you will probably gain a personal understanding of their existence if you take that path. Uranus can offer those lightning flashes of holistic insight which cut through the separative analytical mind, giving access to the unitive dimensions. You should be capable of integrating the spiritual perspective into the mundane material world, thus cross-fertilising the levels and forming an inner balance within yourself. If you do choose to venture along the occult path, then your mental foundation pattern of logic and rationality (Mercury energy) can be of considerable use in moving through layers of illusion and spurious belief thought-forms. Bewitched by the glamour of the exotic and mysterious occult worlds, many fall prey to illusion and an unconscious submission to the occult mystery and authority. They fail to apply the conscious logical mind to the teachings, generally accepting them without serious questioning or personal effort to discover the truth for themselves. Certainly, the rational mind does not have all the answers, and its failure is clearly seen in the world today, but a bridge needs to be established between that level and the more universal holistic perception that Uranus offers, so that the two spheres of mind can work together creatively and harmoniously from the wider conscious perspective. This is a major task for the

Aquarian Age, and one that we are all asked to participate in by
achieving the integration in our own lives.

MERCURY–URANUS SQUARE

The square has several characteristics similar to the opposition. In
both we find eccentric thought-patterns, intellectual superiority,
the 'know it all' syndrome, and a changeability of mind and
emotions which can both confuse and antagonise others.

The main difference with the square's influence is the dominance of the Uranian 'rebel' attitude, which will condition your
social expression. Your initial reaction to most social traditions,
rules, and beliefs will be a belligerent opposition, even if you hide
most of this activity within your own thoughts. A 'rebel of the
mind!'.

There are at least two sorts of rebel: those who just oppose, and
those who oppose and offer radical solutions to social problems.
You are likely to have the tendency to be the 'opposer', as your ideas
are often erratic and impractical, lacking the ability to be easily
applied by people in everyday life. This can be frustrating for you,
but until you come to better terms with contemporary life, it may
be inevitable. Part of this problem is your inability to acquiesce in
social rules and accepted ways of behaviour, allied to an innate
resistance to authority. You fail to see why you have to live in
certain ways, acting and behaving according to a social code of
conduct, or thinking within predictable and conventional parameters. You have enough of a sense of freedom to know that life does
not have to be the way your parents, teachers, employers, politicians and priests tell you. So you become an outsider.

Alienation from society can vary in degree, but you may have to
be careful that your tendency is not just negative in nature, but
possesses a positive creativity for social change. Otherwise it can be
just a pose, an image, a self-indulgence, especially when young.

Responsibility and commitment are two characteristics that you
need to develop.

You may have to realise that the only person who is responsible
for you is yourself! The responsibility for your choices and actions
lies with you, no one else, and it is a foolish denial of personal power
to pretend otherwise, or seek to blame society or someone else for
the repercussions of your choices. It is your life, and your choices

will determine success or failure, enjoyment or suffering.

Your need for self-assertion and uniqueness often causes you to reject well-intentioned advice, without even serious consideration. You do need to listen more to people, because there is usually something of value there for you. Self-preoccupation blinds and deafens you to much in life, and your obstinate insistence on being right can lead to difficulties which defeat even your own objectives.

Basically, what you are looking for is a personal state of freedom. The freedom to live in a world that suits you, and there can lie the problem. How to move from a restrictive world into liberation? One approach is to transfer the energy flow from opposing 'out there' to being turned within, to experience fully the contradictions in your nature, accept them and attempt to resolve or rebalance them. Techniques from the humanistic schools of psychotherapy and creative visualisation could prove useful in this act of re-creation. The social rebel has to undergo an inner revolution. This may be quite difficult, yet it offers the potential to reorientate the energies that are creating problems in your relationships and simultaneously affecting your enjoyment of life. It is a transference from a negativity to a positivity that is to be the aim. You can create a better world to live in if you apply yourself to transforming that inner conflict. You are intelligent and talented enough to use your potential to build a freer world (via relationships, employment changes, etc.), where your choices lead to positive enhancements and increased options for enjoyment. Being frustrated and opposing the world is a waste of time and energy. Determine what sort of life you do want to live, and then find the way to do so; attempting that will absorb your time, energy and commitment in a potentially creative path to your future benefit and for others. Externalise your dream of a new life!

MERCURY–URANUS OPPOSITION

With this opposition, you are likely to experience conflicts in your social relationships. The problem area will be in how you express yourself in communicating with others, and those inner attitudes which condition that style of communication.

Whilst you will have considerable mental vitality, the difficulty will be in directing this into productive channels. The tendency will be towards an erratic inner activity; the nature of your beliefs, ideals and thought-patterns will be changeable, and the attractions of new stimulation will often tempt you away from completing existing projects. The challenge of the new redirects your energy and interests, and so your commitments and responsibilities may feel like restrictive liabilities.

Despite this erratic pattern of mind, you tend to insist that whatever you say and think is valid, even though only a short time ago you were vehemently declaring an entirely opposite attitude, idea or belief. Obviously, this can lead to interpersonal conflict, as most people prefer dealing with relatively stable and consistent individuals, as it helps to develop trust and continuity. Yet if others challenge you by repeating past statements that you have made and are now contradicting, you tend to take offence, often attempting to deny that you ever did say that. Essentially, your reaction is often to deny all prior expressions of your self, refusing to take any responsibility for them. Having experienced this aspect of your nature, many people will begin to draw away from maintaining a relationship with you, because you seem unreliable and difficult to believe. This in a peculiar way reinforces a tendency in you to see yourself as 'unique and misunderstood', which you often use to justify a rejection of social compromise, and you never admit in any circumstances that you are wrong. You appear to project the belief that you 'know it all', and probably succeed more in deluding your self that you do than in persuading others of your expert knowledge.

Underlying these more negative styles of expression is a personality which experiences inner confusion and insecurity, yet attempts to hide this by a superficial image of intellectual superiority. Emotionally, there is likely to be immaturity and lack of ease with that level of your nature, and you are unlikely to touch others easily with the warmth of your personality. This lack of sensitivity and responsiveness to the more intangible 'feeling' aspect of human contact often leads to a tactless and blunt expression, where your ignorance of diplomacy can have negative consequences.

How can you resolve or moderate these challenges within your relationships? The first important step is to acknowledge their presence, to admit that you often are this way. The fact that you may deny them to yourself does not mean that others do not see them clearly. Often, others do see such problem areas, whilst the individual is apparently blind to their existence. They are personal delusions. Being willing to work with people, learning to compromise, and participating as an intellectual equal, will help to moderate these oppositional tendencies. It is a new sense of personal indentity that you should attempt to develop, one founded upon the real you, and not the socially projected assertive one that others may react against. It will involve an acceptance of your inner vulnerability, dissolving that peculiar egotistical construction, and ceasing your attempts to impress people. By stopping that process, you may begin to find your centre, resolve certain conflicts, and redirect the flow of the aspect energy towards personal renewal. Certainly, that inner erratic agitation could be more harmonised and adjusted, thus reducing that build-up of nervous tension from which you suffer.

VENUS–URANUS CONJUNCTION

Aspects made between Venus and Uranus emphasise the spheres of social and intimate relationships, with the energy focus turned towards exploring the outer world through an extroverted personality.

The dominating influence will be the urge for excitement, the stimulation of the unknown and the thirst for the richness of life's experiences. You will not be an introvert, and your main preoccupation will be ensuring that your life is 'interesting', occupying yourself with a multitude of interests and explorations so that there is no time or space left for inner enquiry.

The Uranian influence is the stronger partner of the two, and its agitatory vibration will give you an inner restlessness, which you try to release in social activity and interaction with friends. However, the development of your creative, artistic, unorthodox individuality may lead to adaptation problems in mainstream society, where you react against being employed in mundane, repetitive jobs, or refuse to feel imprisoned in traditional social attitudes, beliefs and lifestyles.

You insist on being free to be yourself, and to do as you please. At times, this can reflect an immature, seemingly adolescent attitude, which can be too self-centred and lack real awareness of others. Also, your definition of your self is inconsistent and dependent on the attractions of the moment. This develops the appearance of unpredictability and lack of continuity, which others often see as a lack of responsibility and commitment.

This will affect your intimate relationships, and you will probably have difficulties in maintaining lasting partnerships, either
because the relationships collapse through a withdrawal of interest, or because there are too many inner desires and conflicts which
trigger stormy, emotionally distressing confrontations. These may
arise because of your insistence upon having your own way, which
can clash with a partner's views, needs and desires. You see your
need for freedom to be important, and so you tend to resist any
attempt to make you give a serious commitment. Your emotions
may only be touched on a superficial level, and rarely fully engaged
with another, which can also lead to periods when you are tempted
to become promiscuous in a search for variety and new experience.
Sudden affairs are quite possible, and also satisfy that urge for
excitement and even danger, where you can express yourself even
more freely than usual. Certainly your love life will have an erratic
quality, similar to the flow of your sex drive, which will confuse
others. Your disdain for traditional forms of relationship can lead
you along many different paths; join this with the fascination that
the unusual has for you, and your life could develop like a multi-
coloured weaving, some colours harmonising, others clashing.

VENUS–URANUS SEXTILE

The Venus–Uranus sextile and trine are easier aspects to deal with,
and both are more socially adaptable. This is because the contacts
between these planets are more diffused, which appears to diminish the more dominating Uranian influence, so that the Venus
characteristics emerge more prominently and are capable of absorbing the erratic Uranian energy. They harmonise more easily,
and the Uranus impact becomes a vitalising enrichment of new
horizons to explore.

You will have a social awareness, which will enable you to have
satisfying relationships with others, which have both a creative and
beneficial effect upon the participants. You will be tolerant in
attitude, and your ability to be sympathetically understanding will
often attract people to confide in you, perhaps using you for personal counselling. Often your innate attitude of acceptance can be
a healing factor in such relationships, and your grasp of life challenges can reveal potential ways for others to resolve their hidden
conflicts. Diplomacy will also come easy to you. This is not a

manipulative diplomacy, but an approach that reflects your natural honesty and sincerity with others, and can be used to resolve disputes.

Your intention is to improve the quality of life, and your social concerns will reflect the futurist impulse of Uranus. Even if you can only achieve harmony within your own immediate environment, then that is a success, and satisfies the impulses of Venus–Uranus, because you know that every oasis of harmony helps to build a better world for all. You are not resistant to compromise with others, because you recognise that it is a positive step bringing people together, and is not a denial of individuality that other Venus–Uranus aspects tend to project within the person. The spirit of compromise is allied to the development of Aquarian group consciousness which uses the energy of goodwill, and if rightly applied releases individual potential and does not restrict its emergence.

In your intimate relationships, you will have a preference for emotional freedom, but because of your other positive qualities, will be less inclined to reach a crisis-point dissolving the relationship in order to secure this freedom. You will tend to work within the partnership to develop mutual trust and interdependence, with the aim of achieving freedom and personal creativity for both, thus turning it into a growth process. Your relationships will have an unconventional dimension, and generally your lifestyle will stand at that point of interface between mainstream traditional society and that of the more iconoclastic, artistic and futuristic groupings. Janus-like, you will perceive both ways, the intermeshing (in harmony and conflict) of the old and the new. Some have to bridge this divide, and you are attracted towards volunteering for this task.

VENUS–URANUS TRINE

The expression of the trine has several similarities to that of the sextile, and usually enables these two planetary energies to work well together.

The social sphere of life will be of considerable importance to you, both as a personal need for contact with others, and in the enjoyment that you derive from it. Whilst you develop your own individuality and style, you have a 'community attitude'; your ideal is to live in a way that both succeeds in satisfying your needs and has a beneficial effect upon the wider world. Your personal values are founded within a social perspective, and you feel that your concerns embrace the world. As a planetary citizen, you may feel attracted towards involvement with those groups which share this attitude, so that either through personal or financial support you are able to contribute towards creating a better world.

The ability to have positive relationships with people may be used through work which brings you into broader contact with the public. This can be through teaching or communication in some way. Possibly your talents can be expressed via artistic creations or music, which embody your Venusian sense of harmony and beauty.

In your intimate partnerships, you find it easy to express your feelings, and these will remain more consistent than with the conjunction aspect. With these Venus–Uranus aspects, though, there is the tendency to be affectionate and sympathetic with the majority of people, a form of diffused love which is universal rather than individually orientated. This can cause some unease and confusion within a partner who fails to be convinced of your specific love for them.

VENUS–URANUS SQUARE

With square aspects, the tendency is for the individual to 'side' with one of the planets, and to partly reject and project the characteristics of the other planet onto other people. It is likely that the more dominating Uranian energy will condition you to the detriment of the Venus feeling nature.

This will be revealed in your insistence upon being emotionally free, and in your reluctance to commit yourself to any single relationship and share in any responsibility arising from that. Part of this wariness is derived from your awareness of a basically promiscuous attitude (whether practised or not), and that often compulsive fascination that can sweep you away on the tides of sudden intense affairs. It is an innate curiosity that tempts you towards those individuals who appear to offer a mystery, something unusual in their life, and you feel the desire to discover and explore their secrets. This does not always lead you into favourable situations, and often can create extra problems in your life, yet you cannot resist the lure of excitement. Once you have uncovered that particular secret, your interest may quickly decline, and you consider yourself to be open to the next fascination that comes along.

You will be socially active, searching for novelty, new people, new interests, and will be especially attracted towards unconventional or artistically orientated groups. You have a natural reaction against convention and social traditions, often dismissing their validity in a quite flippant manner. You tend to see a mainstream, socially acceptable lifestyle as one to be avoided at all costs, and can have a low opinion of those who live that way. To you, it is a denial of individuality to submit to the social consensus, and you consider it important to promote the image of being different. Sometimes you can rebel for the sake of rebellion, to support a less mature image that you aspire towards. You rarely analyse your anti-tradition stance in clear intellectual terms, or express it in the form of a reasoned reaction against certain aspects of society; it is more of an instinctual reaction.

You find it hard to maintain intimate relationships, even when interested in doing so, because part of you is running away from accepting and giving love. Love makes you feel uneasy; you fear that it will inhibit your freedom, and your emotions tend to be repressed to some degree. In extreme cases, the emotions can be almost rigid with inhibition, with a fear of acknowledging and releasing them. Often you experience your affairs or relationships as superficially as possible, enabling you to fly like a butterfly to the next temporary stopping-place. Perseverance is not your strongest asset, and when situations arise requiring self-discipline in order to achieve personal aims, or to maintain a relationship through a difficult phase, you often display that lack of commitment, preferring the excitement of the unknown. You are emotionally fickle, and with that feeling of restless irritation on that level, you may attempt to ignore its presence as much as possible, choosing physical excitement and mental curiosity as your prime directions to follow. As Uranus will distort that feeling nature over time, perverse feelings may begin to form as a kind of twisted inner compensation for an emotional denial. This can lead to unusual and varied sexual behaviour, or the desire to experiment.

In several ways, you probably need to reclaim that Venus feeling part of your nature. Those emotions need to be released, have freedom to breathe properly and to circulate through you. You have to feel those emotions, allow them to penetrate your inner depths, instead of limiting their emergence. Otherwise, over time, they will begin to poison you, affecting any relationships in a negative manner and ensuring that none truly satisfy. Being willing to open to vulnerability in your relationships is essential, to risk being hurt is a chance to take, but can lead to a greater maturation and understanding of the transformative and healing qualities that intimacy can offer.

VENUS–URANUS OPPOSITION

Both the opposition and the square display the stronger influence of the Uranian energy dominating the easier, harmonious social style of Venus. Rebellious unconventional attitudes appear, and with this opposition aspect, you will feel that you have to assert your own unique identity even though it may create discord between yourself and others.

You will often feel disturbed by emotional insecurity and an instability in the consistency of your feelings towards others. In intimate relationships, this will be displayed in swings between red-hot passions and ice-cold disinterest.

This puzzles you, and can obviously confuse a partner, especially when the need for a deeper commitment arises. You wouldn't be sure what to do, and your lover would doubt your real feelings.

Your desires can feel extremely powerful, demanding satisfaction, and the intensity of this energy can lead you to explore unconventional ways of life. A certain impulsiveness and reckless spirit can take you into experiences that could be dangerous, and your choices for relationships may often create future problems for you.

Your unconventional style and basically friendly nature will attract friends, but your own sense of attachment and commitment to them may be erratic. You will be too much drawn by the glamour of following your own unique light to maintain friendships, and some will fall by the wayside as you move ever onwards.

Most of your tendency to oppose will be directed towards authority and those who embody a traditional social structure. As a natural rebel, you will question the foundations of your society, challenge their effectiveness, and probably support the causes of those who are oppressed or disadvantaged by the dominant political attitudes.

You have several characteristics which can be used positively, such as a strong will and determination, and an acceptance of intellectual responsibility (sometimes subverted by emotional instability). The use of these will depend upon your ability to be clear about your objectives, and to maintain enough emotional commitment to fuel your efforts to achieve them.

There is likely to be a need to learn greater compromise and consistency, especially within your intimate relationships, and evoke the Venus energy to a higher degree. Provided that you pay attention, and consider the effects of your choices in life, you will realise that experience will teach you all you need to know, despite its often painful impact. As a rebel, you can learn much about the less publicised frontiers of life, become aware of the heights and depths that people can experience or endure. This will enrich you and increase your maturity. Eventually, you may have much that is of value to share with others.

MARS–URANUS CONJUNCTION

This will give you a dynamic, powerful energy that you attempt to direct in pursuit of your ambitions. One difficulty can be in the often erratic flow of this volatile energy, which creates problems in consistent application. It will seem as though an on-off switch is being internally activated by an unknown hand. This is the unpredictable instability of the Uranian vibration, which is interfering with the drive of Mars.

Even so, the power that you can release is quite considerable, but you may have to learn how to apply it in ways that create the maximum benefit for yourself, perhaps through taking into account this irregular flow pattern, and organising yourself accordingly. When this energy is freely flowing, you will feel highly charged, and under the influence (or 'inebriation') of this energy you are liable to be quite impulsive. Actions can be taken without due thought or consideration, and this can create future difficulties, through following unwise choices. A lack of sensitivity to others, and a diminution of common sense can occur, and you may look for ways to release the sudden pressure that can rapidly build up inside you. In extreme cases, this can be expressed through explosions of temper and anger at any provocation, even to the point of physical violence; certainly attempts to release the energy through verbal and emotionally directed violence towards a partner are common.

You prefer to retain as much independence as possible, and you are not one to bow to any authority. Basically, you are anti-establishment, a natural rebel, an anarchist. You see your own will and desires as paramount, following a purely personal code of behaviour which is determined by a self-centred perspective on life. You tend to insist on your right to be free to follow your own path and ambitions, and can experience relationship problems through this attitude, and may need to learn the values of co-operation to modify this tendency.

Your search for excitement is mainly in terms of physically based action, which can be through competitive sports, or in sexual conquests. You feel a strong need to 'feed' this urge for physical/material level action, and it is tied in with a need to prove yourself in relation to others, to prove that you are better than them in some chosen way.

In some cases, the rebellious spirit can find suitable channels through becoming an opponent of the Establishment, but one who is working from within a socially accepted framework, attempting to change society from within. It may be argued that this is the most effective way, to initiate constructive change through speaking out on behalf of a minority or disadvantaged social group. Irrespective of how you may express this tendency, you will tend to look for results to occur in the physical world as a reflection of your impact. You can have little patience for social rules, preferring to disregard them, but apart from you being penalised if you contravene them, you may have to learn the art of apparent conformity in order to create a foundation that you can work from in your own inimitable, subversive way.

Probably you will find that you become more effective if you can control the inner energy, so that you are able to direct it into predetermined channels of creative expression. The act of clarifying your aims, personal and social, will help this process. Careful consideration of your options and goals will lead to wiser choices at the times of activity, and a gradual transformation from self-preoccupation to becoming more aware of the rights and feelings of others will be a great step for you to make. Learning to share and work with others in co-operation will offer scope for the fullest use of your talents and forceful energy, and will re-integrate you back into society as a positive revolutionary rather than just a negative reactionary.

MARS–URANUS SEXTILE

With the sextile and trine aspects, the more positive use of the Mars–Uranus energy is displayed through activities designed to be of social benefit. Whilst you will intellectually challenge those established patterns of social thought and behaviour which you believe inhibit individual freedom, your intent is to provoke new thinking which can offer the potential of new horizons to explore. All new directions and spheres of progress that humanity has taken have emerged from someone questioning the current static state of affairs and then seeing new alternatives.

Mentally, you will have a restless, curious nature, which can find an effective outlet through applied research and study in whichever areas of enquiry attract you. You are not an intellectual dilettante, and prefer to delve deeply enough to gain a real comprehension of any subject; this can also free that ability for more original independent thinking, and it is possible that you will receive insights that enable you to make a significant contribution to that subject. You will prefer a futuristic dimension to your enquiries, thus satisfying the Uranian impulse and providing an opportunity to benefit others too.

Even though you have this ability for specific focusing, you will also expand into exploring a wide variety of interests and topics. At times you may move rapidly between disparate spheres of knowledge, but will eventually settle down to focus upon one area in particular. You may find some difficulty in perseverance and applying your energy consistently to achieve your aims. Sometimes a sudden diminution of your interest and energy may occur, which brings to a halt any progress you are making. When the energy flows again, you may be interested in something new; this is the erratic Uranian influence.

Communication is important to you. There may be an attraction to teaching in some way, both for the satisfaction you can receive in sharing knowledge with people, and in the platform offered for you to express your opinions. These are likely to be radical and unorthodox, but you have enough intellectual confidence in your knowledge that you feel quite prepared to stand by your arguments against any opponents. Discussions of ideas can fascinate you, and you enjoy such encounters, seeing them as intellectual combat, where your more aggressive Mars energy can be used. Your approach is often based on strategy and skill, and even in friendly discussions you dislike being intellectually defeated. You enjoy stirring dissent, and proposing disturbing concepts and ideas to attack the power of the status quo, both in society and in individuals.

In relationships, you need a strong intellectual and physical bond. An area of weakness can lie in a disregard and lack of sympathetic understanding of the emotions. These are often relegated in your sense of priorities, and the more subtle dimensions of them are ignored in favour of the more basic emotional/physical passions and the interests of the mind. Restrictions are rejected in intimate relationships, and a self-preoccupation can dominate and cause later problems. However, you tend to commit yourself to seeing through those decisions that you do take, so a marriage commitment can help to modify these tendencies, provided that your partner is strong enough to encourage you to modify any selfish behaviour in the interests of mutual harmony.

MARS–URANUS TRINE

With the trine, the Mars and Uranus energies should be reconciled and be capable of working well together. In several respects there is similarity with the sextile, although there will be less emphasis upon the level of mind as a dominating factor.

There will be a multiplicity of interests and fascinating areas of knowledge that will attract you, and you will demand that you have sufficient freedom to be able to explore them. Building upon the results of your studies and skills that you have developed, you will feel attracted towards ways of creativity which demonstrate your capacity for self-expression. Being creative is important to you, and once stimulated you may have the problem of choosing what idea to work with out of the many that appeal to you. Discipline can be ncessary at such a point, where once you decide to follow a creative project, that you succeed in completing it, before diverting yourself into others.

Independence seems necessary for you, and that impatient, restless nature often makes you soon tire of any enclosing intimate relationships. You need a broader scope, with the stimulation of more people to offer more expansive horizons. Group involvements can help to satisfy such needs, as well as providing a focus for your energies. Potentially, you can become a leader of such groups, but if you do so, you may find that your independence becomes constrained and the accompanying duties and responsibilities are onerous. Organisational routines and predictability would limit your freedom – which you would hate. A routine life and employment will not suit you. A greater degree of mobility and choice of activity can be aimed towards building a lifestyle that satisfies your needs, rather than frustrating them. Otherwise, those nervous tensions will grow, and can lead to psychosomatic illness.

If your creative spirit is released, and you enter into a less conventional life, you will find that more unorthodox relationships are appropriate and liberating. A traditional marriage may feel limiting, assuming that this tends to imply a traditional lifestyle as well. Under social pressures to conform, people often find that they are being forced to live in certain ways that are inimical to their natural needs and desires as evolving individuals. Nonconformism is usually penalised, and demands a strong personality to oppose these pressures and so create a life that is appropriate for them. Most societies favour a predictable 'greyness' of population, rather than welcoming a multi-coloured richness that is harder to control.

MARS–URANUS SQUARE

The square will be felt as an inner tension: you are torn between the Uranian search for freedom and a deep need to feel safe and secure. This is a clash between the familiar patterns of the known and the siren call of the potential of the unknown.

This is likely to be felt as a fear of commitment and risk. Whilst you will be attracted towards greater freedom, with the possibility of creating a context where you can be more fully yourself, the likelihood is that you will resist the impulse. As you analyse your options, you prefer to play safe, as you cannot obtain these cast-iron guarantees that you would like as to the future success of your choices. This inner frustration that is likely to build up can cause stress, as a part of your nature is being denied and repressed.

You are liable to feel some emotional unease, where you are afraid of allowing full emotional expression, or even properly acknowledging your emotional nature. It is a fear of 'letting go' that is the root of this difficulty, where emotional or material losses are to be avoided if at all possible. This may have arisen through childhood experiences of loss which deeply affected you, or through a pattern developing that too strongly identified your self with people or possessions, so that with any withdrawal or removal of them from your life, you felt that you were losing part of yourself.

You will feel that you need to keep a tight control on life, trying to ensure that chance and unpredictability are fended off; in this sense, you accept the more grounding energy of Mars, whilst denying the unsettling but potentially liberating energy of Uranus. You apply the Mars energy in terms of conservation, ensuring a protection of your resources through prudent and cautious organisation. You intend to apply yourself diligently to your objectives, even if you expect that they will take longer to achieve without taking risks; the problem is that for varying reasons, your intentions often fail to be realised, perhaps through an impatient Uranus unravelling those attempts at persistent effort. Or your interest wanes as you reach a point where a more risky decisive step has to be taken. When that journey of a thousand miles requires the taking of the first step, you may decide not to travel anywhere, preferring established security.

Yet you may find that you are willing to allow the Uranian impulse to move freely in your life. This could initially arise as a result of a phase of denial where some external circumstance beyond your control throws you into a period of confusion and turmoil. Redundancy or the sudden collapse of a marriage could be triggers for Uranus to break through that dam. Certainly, it will not be denied expression for all your life, and that side of the square will need to be accepted and integrated.

There is the potential that even while maintaining your relative control you could safely begin to open up to new horizons, to explore other interests, to expand and liberate your limiting conception of your nature and life. There are strong foundations there, and you should be able to build efficiently upon them. To achieve those ambitions and personal desires, you will have to take some risks at some point. If you are not committed to achieving them, then it is unlikely that you will ever succeed, because your focus and energy flow will be too diffused and unconcentrated to generate the necessary momentum. That erratic will-power needs to be drawn through into a regular consistent direction. If you can succeed in liberating that inner frustrating tension, you would be surprised how effectively that energy could be applied to reach your aims, instead of clashing within you. Your personal relationships would also improve as the stress began to disperse, and you felt that a great weight was lifting away from your shoulders. Releasing that pent-up, potentially violent energy could mean the dawn of a new era of personal creative enrichment. To free yourself from the restrictions of this square aspect, you have to open up to life's insecurities and risks. It's your choice.

MARS–URANUS OPPOSITION

The energies generated by the opposition aspect are often projected out into the external world, and this will be true in respect of the powerful energy released by this Mars–Uranus aspect. If this is expressed through a more integrated consciousness, which is sure of the direction to travel, then its impact can be considerable. If it is manifesting through a less integrated personality, then it can create real problems in life.

Again, the revolutionary tendency is very strong, and you will have a natural antipathy towards traditions and static patterns of acceptable social lifestyles.

Your attitude will be anti-authoritarian, and you will be iconoclastic in your questioning of the status quo, and critical of those who are in positions of social responsibility and power. Hypocrisy from 'leaders' especially upsets you, and you can be scathing in denouncing it. In fact, you probably have developed a fairly demanding set of personal principles and ideals from which you perceive the world.

You tend to expect less from 'ordinary people', acknowledging their frailties, but you expect the highest standards from social leaders. Concepts of social justice, equality and change attract you, and this can draw you into relationships with revolutionary or reactionary political groups. Depending upon the overall bias of the chart, your radicalism could be directed towards a re-creation of past patterns or a new creation to suit future needs and realities. Generally though, with the Uranian impulse it will be future-orientated, and this will lead you to more altruistic liberal and humanitarian groups.

Your personality can be very assertive, even aggressive and combative. You have an image of yourself 'at war' with whatever you disagree with, whether this is just a war that you fight in your own head, or externalise by opposing social establishments that you dislike. There is a stimulation for you in conflict, and whilst it may not always be openly displayed, you enjoy competition and intend to win and dominate. This is reminiscent of the Scorpio characteristics, which are reflected through this aspect, with the Mars–Scorpio link and Uranus exalted in Scorpio. The quality of assertiveness could be extrovertedly expressed, stridently and powerfully, or quietly through the power of a strong personal presence.

You enjoy arguments and discussions; here the stimulation of ideas, beliefs and attitudes can be enriching. Often you play devil's advocate on ideas, just to enjoy the sparks that can fly, but if it is on a subject close to your heart, then a more passionate, committed side of you emerges, one that is determined to 'win' the argument.

You oppose in principle any restrictions to individual freedoms, although in practice and with serious consideration, you do tend to impose 'limits' for valid social reasons. Your main thrust is towards a broadening of personal freedoms, and the creation of more variety and scope for potential experience and opportunity in life. If discipline is imposed upon you, and you feel that you are imprisoned in a stultifying routine, then you will rise to oppose it; however, for your own purposes you can be highly motivated and self-disciplined.

Freedom is extremely important to you, and is the key to developing your own uniqueness. You feel that you have to get your own way, and this can cause problems if you are too selfish about this demand. If denied, you feel emotionally frustrated, and this becomes a form of pent-up physical tension, which in extreme cases could result in violence. Tendencies to be arrogant, authoritarian and too self-willed can cause friction in social and intimate relationships. If your lifestyle becomes inhibiting, then this can also create explosions of sudden temper and excessive arguing to release inner pressures.

Whilst seeing yourself as an outsider, a loner following a personal path, there is an underlying lack of self-confidence, which Scorpio-like is hidden beneath the mask. You insist on finding and making your own way in life, pursuing one's 'dharma' (own truth), and will be like the traditional stubborn mule if anyone else tries to lead you against your will. You learn from life's hard experiences, and indeed, you tend to accept and welcome such intensity and challenges. Often, you will be tempted to throw off the binding shackles of the past, slough off the old skin like a snake, and burn those bridges to leave yourself free to travel forward into the bright future. You seem as though you know what you are doing, and appear to be optimistic, but this is the glow of a belief in your own ability to succeed, to cross those challenging abysses. You may need to unify your will and clarify your desires so that they work more in harmony.

Potentially, this aspect if rightly applied through a reabsorption of any negative projections back into yourself for transformation, can offer a 'magical' ability to succeed in your aims. The 'enemy' is not just 'out there', and you need to use the tension for self-transformation, to balance out the relationship between yourself and society, so that your revolutionary spirit manifests as an agent for the evolutionary spiral of human progression.

JUPITER–URANUS CONJUNCTION

The expansionary characteristics of Jupiter tend to merge well with the forward-orientated direction of Uranus, and the essential personality outlook should be optimistic and positive. You will tend to believe that there is always 'something good' waiting for you just around the corner, a faith that your future will be rewarding. In some ways, this can become a self-fulfilling prophecy; a positive mental attitude attracts your dreams towards you, enabling their manifestation to proceed more smoothly.

There are likely to be sudden or surprising opportunities arising in your life, which offer the potential of development and expansion. The opening of new horizons can be personal, through relationships and family, educational through further study, or financial and business ventures. You may have to be ready to take full advantage of these, as they can occur sometimes without any conscious effort expended in creating new potential expressions.

You will be very attracted towards exploring human knowledge. You have an avid curiosity, and you believe that all knowledge that you acquire offers more mental freedom and interest, more personal power, and greatly enriches life.

Often, you develop a personal programme for further study in specific spheres of enquiry. This is so you can gain some expertise, so that the information absorbed can be used as a foundation and springboard to launch some kind of project whereby you are able to exploit your own personal potential. You like to create options and alternatives that you could follow, if you so choose, and often mentally build a variety of potential schemes and projects. The problem may lie in being able or willing to actually manifest any of them. Sometimes a fertile mind can circle around a multitude of attractive ideas, yet fail to develop any of them. A more one-pointed discipline may be required.

It is likely that in your quests for expansion and growth you will begin to ally yourself with those more progressively minded people and groups devoted to social change. New political thinking and social alternative lifestyles will attract, especially as your bias will be against the established traditional social order. You will have a reformist outlook, not excessively radical or revolutionary, but still more future-directed than the majority. As an independent thinker, you will serve as an advocate for new horizons in life, and in sowing such seeds, you can help to enrich lives by encouraging others to break free of those limiting, stagnating patterns of life. You welcome the new and unknown; you experience little fear when the winds of change begin to blow, and are ready to embrace their liberating influence.

Jupiter–Uranus Sextile

Both the sextile and trine continue to develop the themes reflected by the conjunction aspect. The natural direction for these merged energies is that of progressive expansion.

The sextile will offer a more definite need to communicate with others. The emphasis on the development of the mind level and intellect, based upon an ever-increasing store of information and knowledge, will be a natural outlet for the energy to circulate in your life. That enthusiastic curiosity and ability to absorb information will be present, although you may need to invest more energy into successfully developing your ideas more clearly and effectively.

Sometimes, in your impulse to rush forward and onward, your impatience can create problems by making you omit to take a crucial step into your considerations. You may need to prepare a little more slowly, using your ability to plan logically and rationally to prevent unnecessary mistakes. It can be like reining back a horse that is threatening to run away with its rider. Unrestricted and uncontrolled expansion can obviously create personal and social problems, and this tendency of Jupiter and Uranus may need to be firmly handled for maximum efficiency. An approach that can successfully utilise the foundations of the past as a base on which to build the future impulse through the mediating influence of the present is the ideal. Burning old bridges and denying the past or present can lead to building upon shifting sands, where hidden, unresolved business can lead to the collapse of the new edifice. You need to aim for an integrated merging.

Teaching can offer a channel of expression, through which your insights and positive optimistic attitudes can communicate the potential of a brighter future to others. This can help to dissolve any tendencies to become overly self-preoccupied and caught in your mental seeking. You believe that there are answers to be found somewhere for everything, and that all obstacles can be overcome. In this characteristic of humanity lies the hope of the future; the quest for answers is the evolutionary impulse at play. It may create an inner discontent and agitation, yet it leads us to progress along the spiral pattern of life towards those new and holistic higher perceptions and intuitions.

JUPITER–URANUS TRINE

The trine offers a relatively easy, free-flowing alignment between these two energies, where again the forward orientation will be evident. You may initially choose to apply your innate talents more for your own personal benefit, but eventually the focus of your outer expression will begin to include ways to improve the quality of life for others too. This may manifest through such spheres of life as education, politics or religion.

You will probably choose to involve yourself with affinity groups that reflect a similar perspective on life to your own; these are likely to be altruistic, liberal, humanistic and radical. Essentially they will be concerned with the quality of life and the improvement of social relationships and planetary stewardship of resources and ecology. These will reflect the Uranus idealism, and combine it with a belief that future expansion for humanity needs to proceed along certain clearly defined paths, which include higher awareness, right relationships and responsibility, individually and collectively.

There should be an ability to work well with groups, provided that your Uranian eccentricity and individualism do not dominate;

potentially, you could serve as a facilitator for such endeavours. You will have a self-confidence and faith in your own abilities, which can be amplified by sudden opportunities which are almost 'presented' to you to take, assuming you are awake to them when this occurs. Looking back over time, it will seem that you have walked a path that has been 'your destiny', a way that is unravelled for you at crucial times, and where there is a sense of inevitability about it.

You will tend to believe that others could be more self-directed, and that if they chose, they could make much more of their lives and talents than they do. This is quite possible, but much of daily life does not naturally encourage such personal development and freedom of choice; for many, their options are quite restricted, especially through economic needs. However, whilst you can appear to succeed relatively easily, there may be a task waiting for you where you can help others to develop their own latent gifts and talents, so making your belief become more real. You will hate any limitation on your freedom, and will react against anyone or any situation that becomes inhibitory or stagnant. Relationships will need to offer you an acceptable degree of personal space.

JUPITER–URANUS SQUARE

There is likely to be a conflict between a need to be externally successful, and an inner struggle to release tensions and transcend limitations. Part of the difficulty will lie in the irregular flow of your energies, which makes it hard to generate momentum and persistence. You will feel that you should be a success, and resent any need to progress slowly in your intended direction. Suitable preparation is not an approach that really appeals to you, yet it can be this failure to lay good foundations that can destroy future success.

You need more clarity in your life. There is a spreading uncertainty within you that makes it difficult to concentrate your energies and purpose together. You are unsure of your real motivations, desires and needs, and there is no cohesive belief structure that you can use as a temporary centre. What you do feel is this frustrating tension, which inhibits your choices and options. Often you make a few steps towards manifesting an intention, make a few preliminary plans, then retreat from this, perhaps from a fear of failure or because a new idea has suddenly attracted all your attention. You have a problem in being self-disciplined and actually completing your intentions. Yet sometimes you can be very impulsive, launching into things with little thought, and suddenly waking up to discover that you have created a new problem or are in a situation that you have to withdraw from. Much energy is wasted through such thrashing about with no real idea of what you really want to do.

The energy to succeed is there, but it is locked away or dissipated through lack of direction. The frustration will remain until you release the tension through channelled intent, completing one project at a time. More self-evaluation as to your dreams and desires will help, as through clarifying those, you will be able to determine the required direction that is necessary for achievement. Those tendencies towards being too idealistic and impractical may need to be moderated, and it may be that you will have to work closely with others in a co-operative manner, so that mutual discipline and focus helps to keep you in line through a sense of group obligation and responsibility. The key is that you need to change your way of operating in order to succeed.

JUPITER–URANUS OPPOSITION

Most of the challenges that are likely to face the individual with this aspect will be centred on personal beliefs and expression, and relationships with others.

You are likely to have a bright, alert, intellectual mind, and a sense of self-assurance which can be expressed with enthusiasm and dynamic energy. Over time you will amass a large storehouse of knowledge, which you can use in your efforts to become successful and creative. What is likely to disrupt the results of such natural assets is the influence of the Uranian opposition, which essentially distorts the outer expression.

It is in the spheres of judgement and sensitivity that you may find difficulties occurring. Under the expansionist tendencies of both Jupiter and Uranus, you can easily become over-enthusiastic about ideas, business schemes or unconventional beliefs. Allied to an erratic, restless tendency, this can lead you to become involved in highly speculative business ventures where your obsession with the project idea can override any real rational analysis of financial feasibility. Often your attachment to ideas veers towards investing them with elements of fantasy and imagination, which can lack a real applicability within daily life, also adding a distorting factor.

There is likely to be some conflict with established traditional beliefs and social attitudes, especially in the areas of religion and politics, and you may become involved with radical politics or more unusual religious and spiritual beliefs. These will hold considerable personal meaning for you, and you will feel impelled to share these with others. Often despite that clever mind, there is an element of simplicity and faith in you, which can become naïvety at times. If a belief resonates with that point of imagination within, you can accept it then with little questioning, because really you are looking for a sense of centre and security, and a belief structure appears to offer this.

You may need to be wary of an urge to convert others to your beliefs which, whilst genuinely held, may not be suitable for everyone. If others oppose you, this serves to reinforce your support of your beliefs against any odds; you can feel that this often validates them. There can be a tendency to be too domineering in expression, founded on that strong self-assurance, and in relating there is often a lack of tact and sensitivity to the feelings and abilities of others. Not everyone has your ability to be so focused on achieving objectives; many vacillate, or sit on the fence, instead of choosing to be on one side or the other. Also, others have different requirements for life experiences than you, different challenges for different folks, and they may be following their path as much as you are.

Eventually, you may find that the Uranus action causes you to revolt against any belief structures to which you have bound yourself. At least for a period, you may have to stand alone and adrift from security in beliefs; this can occur as a result of disillusionment and a collapse in your faith in a specific belief. Yet this can be liberating, as in the experience of such a phase of inner darkness, your own light may be perceived and contacted, enabling you to live more freely and attuned to your own life pattern through later life. Identification with outer belief structures can be personally inimical and restrictive.

SATURN–URANUS CONJUNCTION

During this century, the conjunction aspect has been made during

1942 and in 1988. It offers the possibility of an effective balance between these two antagonistic planets. Apart from those born under this aspect, the energy released into the collective mind at these times can aid in the interplay between forces of order and chaos, conceivably bringing the opposites into equilibrium and allowing a space for something new to be born.

For the individual with this aspect, there should be the ability to fuse ideas with practical application, to ground and anchor those sometimes slightly intangible and ephemeral Uranian ideas, thus transferring them from the level of mind into material existence. You should be able to take advantage of your personal resources and talents, and these can be effectively expressed through efficient organisation. The flow of Uranian energy should seem more consistent and reliable, and you will be able to apply persistence and focused will to achieve your objectives. Often, you will find enjoyment from becoming involved in situations where you can create order from chaos. Whilst this may appear Saturnian in nature, Uranus is not chaotic for the sake of it, but is only disruptive in order to create the conditions for a higher order to be superimposed.

You can function in a 'bridging role', carefully restoring a balance between order and change, and re-integrating this into a new structure which is an improvement on the previous one. In modern life, where so many changes are occurring so quickly, such a role can be most important, and utilises both of these planetary characteristics in a positive way. You have a sympathetic understanding of the past, and of the values and attitudes of conservative stability, yet also intuit and appreciate the necessity of change and evolving of social structures, organisations and individual development. You will try to integrate these threads, uniting what is worth retaining from the past with the ideas of the next step forward. Doing this, you work with both your intellect and intuitional faculties, and so reflect the next stage in human development towards the consciousness of unity.

You are likely to prefer a form of expression that involves a social contribution over and above mere participation in society; you would like to feel that you have some influence in improving things, and that your preoccupation is not totally for personal gain. This need can often give you a sense of direction in your life, and one which can absorb both of these planetary energies. If you begin to feel that you are having to keep down inner pressures of certain kinds, perhaps through a lack of channels to release them into, then it is a likely sign that you are not fluently expressing both the energies. Look at your life pattern and see which one is being repressed. In most cases, this would be the Uranus energy, as the Saturn energy, which is one of order and discipline, is often expressed through social conditioning. To free this blocked energy, more spontaneity, more experimentation, and exploration of new interests would help. These would stimulate needed changes to happen and so break down any fixed lifestyle patterns that are becoming inhibiting. If the Saturn energy is repressed, more self-discipline, commitment and perseverance to achieving your objectives would help. If the lifestyle lacks control, too much freedom could also lead to a loss of a personal centre and stability, leaving you feeling lost and unsure of what to do or in which direction to travel. You will need to draw through the Saturn qualities of boundary-making and structure, so that your life and inner nature begin to take distinct form again, creating a stable foundation to work from.

Saturn–Uranus Sextile

The Uranus attraction towards ideas finds fluent expression with this aspect, where there is the ability to make use of all information and knowledge that has been gained through education and experience. You will enjoy mental stimulation and intellectual pursuits, and have a high regard for the human development of mind, giving it precedence in importance, especially when it can have practical application. There may be some diminution of emotional expression, as you try to override the needs of that level, perhaps in an attempt to be rational and logical in your relationships. Some rebalancing may be necessary to prevent emotional repression and energy blockages.

You will probably have an approach which searches for and collates all necessary information that you need either for a practical project, or in order to become informed and capable of forming a personal opinion about a specific topic. You believe that decisions should not be based on ignorance or emotional reaction, and so you intend to acquire sufficient knowledge to allow freedom of decision and choice. This is part of the general efficiency and organisation that you are proud of, and this, allied with a sense of self-confidence and the ability to be assertive, allows you to make full use of your natural talents.

'As with the conjunction, you are likely to feel able to contribute towards group work, with those associations of people that you feel are in mental affinity with you and perceive the world in similar ways. There will be that ability to perform a bridging role, where a channel of communication can be established between those reflecting established patterns of thought and attitude, and those who are struggling to clarify and express the meaning of the emerging new world order. With an appreciation and attraction to progressive ideas, yet also recognising the value of the old and need for some stability within change, you can be effective in blending the two approaches and helping to form a viable foundation on which long-lasting development can be built. In your own right, you can contribute to the birth of the new through acting as a channel for original and inspired ideas, which you are able to ground through an ability to relate them into practical terms and by using common sense in knowing how much can actually be achieved now. You recognise that some inspiring ideas can be anchored now, whilst others require considerable changes to occur both in people and society before they can succeed. Understanding this, you will choose to work with only those that are capable of being actualised now, knowing that in succeeding with these, you are building the firm foundation for future transformatory ideas to materialise later.

Saturn–Uranus Trine

The trine aspect can offer a good working balance between these two energies, one which can successfully reconcile their opposing natures. The more positive Saturn qualities allied to less extremist Uranian ones will be in evidence, operating through your personality expression.

As with the conjunction and sextile aspects, the trine will enable you to anchor and materialise the Uranian impulse, so that the energies will flow easily and fluently through you without creating any unnecessary blockages. Working from the Saturn ability of self-discipline, practical skills and organisation, you can take full advantage of the inspirational ideas of Uranus, eventually making them real on this material level. Yet you are not dazzled by materialism, and much of your actual interest and enjoyment is with the nature of the ideas themselves; being capable of manifesting them to some degree is but a completion of the process. It is those futuristic ideas and dreams that take hold of your imagination, giving it some form, definition and direction.

You are able to learn quickly from life experiences; you choose not to waste time having to repeat similar experiences through failing to realise the implicit lessons hidden within them. Time is short, and you prefer to make the best use of your natural talents and resources for yourself, and to aid others too if the opportunities present themselves. Potentially, you could become an inspiration for the young and others in how to actualise your intentions and complete the process of creativity, due to your ability to resolve the Saturn–Uranus polarity. Much of human experience revolves around the conflicts inherent in that dualistic polarity, and you could become an exponent of the fact that it can be reconciled. Your life could demonstrate the ability to weld together old and new impulses, the creative process, and the dichotomy of matter–spirit. Obviously, it would not always be easy, but you can make the potential real in your life, and prove to others that it is achievable. This is another aspect of the 'bridging role and function' that is currently needed during this transition stage, when unifying the planetary impulses is essential.

Saturn–Uranus Square

The main theme of this square is the likely dominance of the Saturn qualities and a repression of the Uranus ones, with a personality expression being restricted by responding to the Saturn viewpoint on life.

This will be seen in a preference for the familiar and known, both in a ready acceptance of social convention (which in its reactionary phase is often rooted in a backwards-looking perception of a 'return to a golden age'), and in the desire for a personal life lived in a controlled, predictable manner and in a stable environment. The personal identity will be focused within strictly defined parameters, with self-imposed limitations on freedom of choice and action, wrapped around with concepts of allowable thoughts, emotions and physical acts. Much of this is a protective guard against the actual insecurity of life, and emerges from a personality that is afraid to relax fully and which is inwardly insecure.

Difficulties may arise in life when attempting to solve problems by applying existing attitudes which then fail to work. You often find the need for change deeply disturbing, and have an intuitive fear thàt if you allow that process to occur, then your life would fall apart. When you have to make decisions regarding new situations, you can find it hard to make a final choice, unless you discover a way to do so which reinforces your existing attitudes and preferences; if it involves a new direction, then you become uneasy, trying to find a way to retreat back towards your old familiar patterns.

In those attempts to impose control on life, you can be too dictatorial or authoritarian in your relations with others, perhaps through an insistence upon your point of view being right, or in having everything done in an established manner without deviation. Your life can become very predictable and highly patterned, locking you into a circumscribed experience of life. This can define your identity for you, offering a way for you to evade those feelings of insecurity and lack of real confidence, but this will restrict you taking advantage of many opportunities in life. Often, you seek social status or approval in order to gain a reflected sense of self-worth.

Denying the Uranian vibration of change can lead to problems of life adaptation and inner tensions, especially as there will be an underlying struggle between an affinity with traditional patterns and an attraction and fear of something new being released into your life. Saturn will embody the more inflexible end of the square, and if you begin to respond to Uranus (or a transit stimulates its activity), then these inhibiting patterns will begin to be eroded and destroyed. Part of you – a repressed aspect – would secretly love to break free of all binding ties, to become unconventional and liberated; if the pressures rise too strongly, then attempts to throw off self-imposed shackles may be made, just to release the tensions. Marriages and careers can be destroyed through such activity, with the end result being a collapse of existing patterns with no real comprehension of how to build a more suitable lifestyle, and just a feeling of an inner void and loss of direction being common. Ongoing transformation is the wisest course of action, as the transitions move more smoothly and the person is capable of slowly adjusting to new ways in a more harmonious manner, integrating the arising new tendencies more successfully and easily.

Even within those Saturnian confines, the Uranian undercurrent is at work. The operation of your mind – where you focus yourself in order to control life – is more inconsistent and contradictory than you believe. Others probably notice this, but you will oppose any attempts to point this out to you, in your belief in your logic and rationality. Yet in the background of your mind lurk those more eccentric ideas, thoughts, desires and emotions that you rarely acknowledge. Sometimes, the strains of living with denied aspects can make you touchy in relationships, where people have to treat you in certain ways so as to avoid 'triggering those buttons' which stimulate areas in you that you choose not to explore. For real health, these need to rise into the light, so that the pressures and energies can be released, and that you can integrate parts of your being. If you choose not to, it is likely that at some point in life, Uranus will erupt with a vengeance, and sweep away all those pretences, patterns and controlled lifestyle, forcing you to confront your denied selves and to change.

SATURN–URANUS OPPOSITION

With the opposition, you will tend to project inner tensions outwards onto others through your social and intimate relationships. These tensions arise as a result of the clash of the Saturn and Uranus energy patterns within you, and will continue to remain operating until you succeed in resolving the causes of the inner friction, through transforming the relationship of Saturn–Uranus.

You may feel torn between two polarised directions, past–future, order–chaos, orthodox–unorthodox, stability–change. This may make it difficult for you to decide on life directions, or you may become biased towards one pole to the repeated exclusion of the other, and some degree of repression will occur of the ignored planetary qualities. This can give you a hard edge to your personality, which is partly a result of trying to maintain a fixed inner centre against the other inner planetary attraction. You prefer to remain clearly in control, but can express this with what seems to others an overly agressive approach.

There can be a lack of relaxed relationships, perhaps because you have a competitive attitude and desire to become personally important and authoritative in a social sense. It is doubtful if you will have many close friendships, because of an attitude of exclusion and distancing that you erect around yourself.

One area that can create conflict for you is a lack of openness to others, and that attitude of righteous knowing; this can block any real relationship occurring, and often will generate antagonism from others, who look for opportunities to 'bring you down'.

Learning to listen more to what others have to say is one lesson you need to apply; there is something of value to be gained from communication with every person, because the wisdom of the whole is reflected through each individual, and the routes that guidance and messages can take are infinite in variety. If you are not open to the world and people, you will miss them, and just circle around in your own limited world. Life can be greatly enriched by sharing with others in an attitude of equality. Co-operation and compromise should then flow by such an adjustment in your attitude to others, as you break down that restrictive egocentric shell.

It is likely that the Uranian energies will be less expressed than the Saturnian ones, so some degree of rebalancing may be required to free that planetary influence. This can be released through personal creativity and allowing yourself to be more free and less tightly bound. This can involve the dissolution of limiting self-images, and an inner granting of freedom to others, so that you do not insist that they conform to your image of them. Often you attempt to direct their lives for them, especially in the more personal sphere of relationships, because it makes you feel able to control life. In the way that you are applying this, the results just inhibit a vibrant life.

The Uranian characteristics can also emerge if you become involved in social reforming groups, where you may release that aspect of your nature in an active manner through questioning the Establishment. What you may have to be wary of is a bias towards Uranus that leads to losing the awareness of the essential Saturn values in life. What you should be aiming towards is a way to create a workable balance between these energies within your own nature and through relationships, so that the positive aspects of each can shine through.

NEPTUNE–URANUS CONJUNCTION

The conjunction aspect occurs quite rarely; the last was around 1821–1823, and the next will be in 1992–1994, allowing a 2 degree orb. Aspects involving the transpersonal planets focus more on the generational and social dimensions of life, where the attitudes and experiences of the individual are intimately linked with social changes.

Nobody currently alive has this aspect, but a new generation who will be born in the early nineties will demonstrate these characteristics as they mature. There will be a strong degree of identification with the collective mind and group consciousness, which in some cases could revert back to fervent nationalist affinities in countries that have a powerful controlling religious, racial, political and social structure. Yet in most cases, it is unlikely that this will result in the emergence of charismatic demagogues as in recent examples of manipulation of the masses.

There will be a directing sense of social responsibility, and an awareness of participating in a social community, which will be expressed in positive ways for the betterment of all. The merged energies of this conjunction will inspire concepts of brotherhood which reflect the ideals of Uranus and Neptune, as a form of revolutionary mysticism emerging from an acute mental and emotional sensitivity connected to an intuitive imaginative faculty.

Personal freedoms and rights have a high priority, and there will be a new perception of 'leadership' being formed, which can dissolve those old patterns of a powerful leader and hundreds of following 'sheep'. There is a distrust of leaders, based on an intuitive perception of their real motivations and characteristics, which will also develop into a new understanding of authority and power in society. Those born under this aspect, will be willing to 'fight' for the maintenance of personal freedoms and rights if they are under threat by the decisions of social leaders. A new balance of power between the people and the State will begin to form, and a new politics should rise into view that reflects the increase in individual rights and power. Generally, this should be a period of spiritual and scientific development, where breakthroughs occur in the exploration of nature and mind.

As these planets conjunct in 1992–1994, at a time which will see the birth of the generation that will become socially influential during the period when Pluto is in Aquarius and Pisces at the end of that transit cycle, it is expected that signs will emerge then that point to the new world which this new generation will inherit. Changes that will become inevitable by 1994 will have to be more fully achieved and realised by that future generation, imbued with a more conscious spirit of human unity and solidarity.

NEPTUNE–URANUS SEXTILE

Most of the characteristics of Uranus–Neptune aspects involve the element of distrust for leaders, organisations and power élites. Those born with the sextile aspect tend to object to establishment secrecy and the withholding of information from their people or electorate. They consider this manipulation of information to be a deliberate and iniquitous distortion of the truth which should not be allowed by their leaders. Often such people would support a 'freedom of information' cause, believing that the State should be the servant of the people, and not the other way round.

There is an anti-establishment attitude, together with an objection to State autonomy in which the individual is steam-rollered by the weight of the State bureaucracy. There is a need to reassert individual power and freedom from State interference, and such attitudes will often oppose authoritarian dictates. An attraction towards social revolution and changing the nature of State control can develop a revolutionary philosophy which champions the people's right to power within their own society.

An optimistic belief in people and their potential will dominate, which some may consider to be too naïve and idealistic, but it is founded on the right to be able to choose for oneself, and to determine the sort of personal lifestyle to live without being inhibited by social repressions (provided that it does not harm others). It conceives of a society geared towards personal development and fulfilment, through individual creativity and uniqueness, in contradistinction to one which conditions people to unquestioning fulfilment of economic roles and adherence to social convention.

Essentially, it asserts the right to be self-determining, rather than meekly and blindly following the guidance of leaders who often gain their positions through money or inheritance alone. An active involvement in social decision-making will attract, especially in ways designed to make some progress towards those brotherhood ideals which so appeal to the mind and emotional levels of those with this aspect.

NEPTUNE–URANUS TRINE

The trine aspect was made during 1941–1946 approximately, and features in the birth-charts of a generation born during war-time.

This tends to condition their perception of life and people, which can sometimes veer towards pessimism and cynicism, especially if they were born in the early years of the trine when the war was at its height and the result still hung in the balance.

Underlying this is still the idealism of these planets, but with possibly insufficient personal faith in their actual manifestation, together with an ambiguity about their own personal role and responsibility in society. There can be a tendency to follow personal goals irrespective of social needs and obligations, and a preference for personal gain and ambitions. Yet this too can be a source of personal unfoldment, and it is still perhaps too early yet to be sure how such individuals will use any social power and influence that they may have acquired.

As the trine is a reconciling factor, this generation could be seen as a 'bridging group' where both the past and future tendencies co-exist, probably uncomfortably at times. They have grown up in a rapidly changing world, whilst childhood conditioning would still reflect pre-war attitudes, and are able to serve as mediators in society, knowing the older world yet attuned enough to the dawning of the new.

There should be sufficient intellectual capacity to evaluate the implications of ideological belief structures for themselves, without the imposition of authority, resulting in the development of genuinely held personal views irrespective of their nature and content. Unless they feel convinced of the validity of an idea or belief, after having considered it carefully, they will usually be unable to give whole-hearted support for it – unless they compromise themselves for personal gain.

They are aware of the dangers of a lack of public discrimination and gullibility regarding leaders – as the German people in World War II demonstrated – yet are not fully convinced by the intent of any leaders who use truth as an expediency to be employed only when it suits them.

In many ways, this generation is faced with a need to resolve certain inner conflicts and opposite world-views, almost as a 'trial run' for the way that society can achieve this on a larger scale. There are paradoxes on both mental and emotional levels that should be resolved and integrated, because too often such people are caught on the cleft stick of their own indecision and confusion over which 'face' to present; the face of the older ways, or the face reflecting the emerging changes in the world.

NEPTUNE–URANUS SQUARE

The last square aspect happened during 1952–1956, and influenced the people born during that phase. These were the second phase of post-war children, born into a time of relative stability and reconstruction, when the memories of the war were ebbing away into past history, even though the Korean War was rekindling some of them.

This group received a psychic impression from the collective which embodied a form of social confusion which was prevalent and reflective of the collective mind. Social direction was the issue. The defeat of Churchill's government after the ending of the war, a government which seemed now to represent the past, and the introduction of post-war Labour reformist policies like the Welfare State, seemed to herald a new vision and direction. But the collective was torn between dreams and fears of a new world, and a rejection of painful recent memories of man's inhumanity; a clash between the future and the past, the unknown and the known.

Reflecting this collective conflict, the individuals born at this time received a pattern of rebellion (Uranus) which was mixed with confusion (Neptune) over what to do, what direction to travel in, how to achieve objectives, even what these objectives actually were. The only model that could be absorbed was that of their parents and peers, which offered conflicting and confusing social messages.

The problem in later life would be ambivalence; they would be torn between a need to revolt against authority and the Establishment, and a need to feel socially secure. Purity of idealism would become a challenge, especially when confronted with the pragmatic demands of economic and family life.

With this aspect, there is an aversion to leaders, who, it is felt, lead people into blind obedience and conformity, which to the Uranian spirit is anathema, and opposed to the Uranian principle of freedom. Personal freedoms are paramount, and their repression may lead to a struggle to assert them. Yet this group eventually fragmented into various types. Some were reluctant revolutionaries, eventually being reabsorbed into the social mainstream, some were 'rebels without a cause', social misfits with no direction except that of aggressive reaction. Members of this aspect group were attracted to the existing hippie and drug counter-culture, in the later phase after 1968; others became early leaders of the mid-seventies punk movement, an anarchic reactionary youth revolt against conformity; and perhaps most of all, the spreading of the New Age movement, which incorporates the ecological Green political groups.

In fact, many of those who were early adherents of the hippie ideals have become part of the New Age culture, which is expanding throughout society, through alternative health therapies, mind training, healthy foods, and an ideology of individual and collective wholeness. It is in this way that the core group of those born during 1952–56 are active in taking control of their own lives and influencing society.

NEPTUNE–URANUS OPPOSITION

Like the conjunction aspect, the opposition is made approximately every 171 years. The last one was during the period 1906–1910.

What seems to occur with this aspect is a domination of the conscious mind by a social conditioning programme, which makes the individual and the collective less aware of what is actually happening in the collective mind. The transpersonal planets stimulate an agitation in the unconscious, so that areas requiring release and resolution are brought out into the open through encountering crisis.

It is a phase when the conscious mind is absorbed within the status quo, firmly fixed in its world-views, ideologies, religious beliefs and social lifestyles. Basically, life is running along clearly defined 'tracks', with relatively little questioning or dissidence; yet under the superficial calm, there is brewing a maelstrom of repression and restricted energy searching for release and expression. In many ways, the individual is too identified with collective groups, and is losing the ability of self-determination and freedom of choice. This involves a relinquishing of personal responsibility, and transfers collective power into the hands of those who volunteer (for various reasons) to be social leaders.

There is likely to be a misplaced optimism and illusions concerning the well-being of society, because the dynamic of change and the struggle to achieve a high ideal is being denied full expression. Inwardly, both within the individual and the collective, there is a conflict between the emotional and mental levels, as there is no real meshing under the directing influence of a focused will. It is as

thóugh a comfortable pattern has been established, which is con-
formed to with little discriminatory awareness. There is mental
tranquillity, but this somehow denies a satisfying emotional dimension, which turns that energy within to fester. Eventually it will
re-emerge as motivation, creating mind desires which will generally embody a separatist attitude. This was seen in the nationalist
and economic greed that emerged prior to World War I, and was
even repeated in the later war of 1939–1945.

This can be a confusing phase, in which the real activity is stirring
underneath the surface, ready to erupt. The individual becomes
swept along by major social changes, and real choices eventually
have to be made as a consequence of confronting the results that
emerge from the inner tensions. Sides have to be taken, and instead
of apathy, a real struggle can ensue in the attempt to secure the
preservation of the essentials of the State lifestyle against potential
aggressors, who could be either internal or external. Yet change
cannot be ignored, and a revolution of some kind will happen. Two
examples of this are the Russian Revolution, and the World Wars,
both of which led to permanent international change.

PLUTO–URANUS CONJUNCTION

The aspects of Uranus to Pluto tend to be socially and generation-
ally orientated, and the qualities, tendencies and attitudes associated with them are those which give a distinct conditioning tone to
society during the period of the aspect.

The conjunction is quite rare, being made the last time around
1848, a time of social revolution in Europe and a time of great civil
unrest and social change in Europe and America, and occurring
again in the period of 1963–68.

The influence of these potent transpersonal planets is likely to be
radical and far–reaching, setting a trend for the following century
to develop and integrate, one which requires a long period of time
for society to assimilate. In that sense, the influence is world-wide,
and the period in which the close conjunction is made should be
carefully analysed to perceive the essential thrust of this directive
energy and the emergent trends for social development over the
next hundred years.

With the cosmic periodic releasing of such powerful energies,
the human reaction to them is varied and often polarised in re-

sponse. These reveal the interface between the individual life and the collective life of a society. It is as though from a multiplicity of sources a new alluring voice is rising, which is revealing a new approach to life for society to absorb. Certain individuals respond enthusiastically to this new siren call, embracing 'the new way', and begin to group together as an influential minority within their own society. They then reflect the new ideas, impregnate society with them and act as transmitters of change. Broader social reaction to 'the new way' is often slow, apart from the inevitable reaction against the new trend, and often society attempts to use the power of its established structures to resist what appears to be a threatening impulse.

The influence of the conjunction is to initiate a new phase of social change, and during the 1963–68 aspect, it is that of a revolutionary new spirit in the air, extolling the virtues of individual rights and freedom, stimulating the need for the transformation of the existing social establishment and the breakdown of outdated and limiting social and national attitudes and engrained patterns of thinking.

For those who were (and still are) attuned and receptive to this visionary energy, there is a personal feeling of involvement in a vast process of evolutionary development occurring on earth, a feeling that their individual life is intimately linked with a vast plan slowly unfolding into manifestation, and that their lives are guided by some greater consciousness, participants in a planetary drama. As a world-wide group held together by shared response, they collectively form a conduit for the new social approach to be mediated into human life and consciousness. Some reflect this in a more conscious manner, by seeking to manifest the overshadowing energy via deliberate meditation or occult rituals, etc.

What is of importance to this group is the respect and value for life in all of its forms, ranging from human life to animals, plants, all of the many appearances of Nature and the abundant creativity of Earth. Life is viewed as essentially 'holy', to be cherished, respected, enjoyed and protected. It is a basic attitude to life that wants the highest quality of life for everyone, founded upon a balanced and careful relationship with the environment and the natural world, whereby human society moves from being a dangerous exploiter of nature's gifts to living in a more natural harmony. Individually, there is the need to develop as a unique person, free to live and express oneself within a peaceful, co-operative coexistence, to learn how to unfold innate potentiality without it infringing on the rights of others.

Viewing the world situation some twenty years after the close conjunction, the attitudes released into the world at this time are still serving as a necessary social direction, and many pressure groups have been formed to further the progress of such causes. The succeeding century needs to see more development for the benefit of mankind.

PLUTO–URANUS SEXTILE

The sextile aspect occurred in the midst of World War II and it could be considered that the nature of the energy released during 1942–1946 was a positive boost to the Allied forces at the time, as it stimulated their cohesiveness and commitment to fight against the oppressive Nazi regime.

If actually applied in the world, the tendencies which are associated with this sextile would help bring about social improvement and clarity within government and publicly representative bodies.

It invokes a natural voice of the people to object against social injustice and hypocrisy, to resist dictatorial abuses of power and influence emanating from central government, and to expose corruption wherever it occurs in high places. It embodies the dichotomy between the individual and the State, wherein the State should reflect the democratic will of the people, and be the elected servant of the people, and yet in real life becomes an independent entity dominated by power-blocs and influential political parties which perceives itself to be superior to the people and often ignores their demands. The political élite is often quite dismissive of the general public, believing that it has the machinery and power to manipulate the social consciousness as it wills, and invariably wishes that what often passes as democracy did not exist to get in its way.

Unfortunately, the analysis of public apathy and the élite's ability to manipulate social attitudes is often correct, and serves as a reactionary barrier to social progress. However, one tendency of this aspect is to expect and insist upon a high quality of governmental leadership, a belief that those in positions of authority and social influence should express the highest ideals, morals and values of the society they represent; if not, they should be replaced. A shift in this direction, assuming such quality people made themselves available, could stimulate a major change in society; it is a prerequisite for the new vision to appear in the future. Preserving and expanding the nature and depth of freedom in the world is an ongoing struggle, in the West as in the East, as there are many who wish to see it destroyed for self-centred reasons.

Of interest during these war years was the rapid development of the Manhattan project, and the birth of the atomic bomb, which demonstratedthe sudden 'lightning flash' quality of Uranus both in the scientific intuitions and insights needed to create the technology and in the physical demonstration of its effect. This links with Pluto's negative social face, which confronts us with a choice of two forms of transformation, negative and positive, collective destruction or collective unifying change. The way forward obviously depends on public activism or apathy, and on the quality of social leadership and the nature of the conditioning attitude, separatist or unitive. Thus the circle turns to confront us with those tendencies associated with the sextile aspect, which collectively, we are still facing.

PLUTO–URANUS TRINE

The trine aspect occurred during the 1920s, and stimulated an impulse of international change, the urge to reform existing social and political structures. The acknowledgement of the necessity of this is displayed in the economic instability and collapse in America and Germany, the British Depression and the initial creation of the new Communist regime in Russia. In addition, new political approaches emerged as Fascism, National Socialism, Communism, all founded on 'new' ideals and ideologies, and yet all often demonstrating an outlook liable to cause international conflict, despite their domestic social improvements benefiting their own people.

Change was in the air; many were responding to its heady effect, trying to take advantage of the energies recently released to them, and there is a feeling of a searching and experimentation during a time of crisis and transition, when little seemed clear and definite, and most seemed part of an international melting-pot, the results of which could define the direction of the future.

There was an acceptance of breaking free of the past, becoming open to all new ideas and developments; some welcomed this with excitement, as cultural and social structures began to dissolve or lose their predominant places, some found the changes disturbing, feeling the sands beneath their feet changing too rapidly to feel secure. Those under the trine's influence felt that the tide of history was moving with them, and that no obstacle could stand in their way for long. The traditional ways were considered outdated and restrictive, and they were looking for something new in which they could discover some form of personal meaning, and they flocked to support the new emergent political philosophies with emotional enthusiasm, as they appeared to embody the new world that they felt was imminent.

The Uranus–Pluto trine acted as a channel for energies to stimulate national characteristics, and to dissolve the power of tradition and the past. It had a jarring effect on the world, initially received as what can now be perceived as a destructive and deluding force, yet one which was necessary to clear the ground for the more constructive influence to emerge. It gave a boost to scientific and intellectual development in the West, yet stimulated a relatively immature emotional level in society, which found early security by becoming part of mass emotional support for those charismatic demagogues that rose to the forefront of the political arena. In some ways, the effects of the trine are the direct opposite to those of the previous opposition aspect at the turn of the century, 1900–1903, almost as if the 'turning of the screw' creates even more social confusion and conflict within the period of the World Wars. Certainly the changes occurring within this twentieth century have been profound and extensive, a rapidly moving series of crises developing in every aspect of life, perhaps leading towards some epochal crescendo.

PLUTO–URANUS SQUARE

The influence of the square aspect was to stimulate 'destructive' social change across international borders, to intensify all those latent nationalistic characteristics that had been coming to the surface of the national group minds, until the only way to express and release the underlying tensions was through world conflict.

The close square applied from 1931 to 1934, and the phase was of rapid metamorphosis in crucial countries like Germany and Italy. These were two clear examples of the impact of the

Uranian–Plutonian energy, where nationalistic tendencies and élitist attitudes were elevated into a sense of social direction, manipulated by dictatorial groupings in an attempt both to seize power and to benefit the State by introducing new political concepts. The power complex and need to dominate of the unregenerated Pluto energy is displayed in the need to expand their control and influence into other less powerful nations, through ruthlessly expressed violence and force.

The general world economic instability helped to create the space for radical and revolutionary political agitators to gain power, feeding off the exploited energy of will (Pluto) to build an apparently attractive edifice of the new society. In many cases, this basic urge to create new social structures was genuinely held by those whose motives and ideals were socially beneficial; however, they were to lose their positions of responsibility to those whose intentions were more mixed, and who were being swept along by their receptiveness to the powerful energies pouring into the world, which served to over-stimulate aspects of their unintegrated personalities.

The collective group responding to the Fascist and Nazi ideals were generating and reflecting the possessing energy, especially through the group mind and seen in those emotionally manipulated and invocative mass public rallies, which were similar in effect to certain types of magical ritual. There were two main ways in which people reacted to the social change occurring. One was to collaborate with it, being excited and thrilled by active participation in a national resurrection, irrespective of some of its hidden darker aspects. The other way was to be apathetic and passive, allowing it to go on all around them, feeling insecure and unable to have any influence even if they disagreed with the dominating group.

What became paramount in this square, was the stimulation of the unconscious national mind and emotions by Pluto, which overrode the more intellectually idealistic mind quality of Uranus. All those repressed tendencies rose into physical view, those attitudes of superiority, of national frustration, of harsh, sadistic dismissal of other 'inferior' races, and of the power of violent aggression became integrated into the expression of the new society, and freedom was ignored by the might of the oppressor. The dark face of incorrectly applied Pluto energy was ready to be unleashed onto the world.

PLUTO–URANUS OPPOSITION

At the time of the opposition, in 1900–1903, social traditionalism in the West was at its peak, and feeling that it was culturally advanced and essentially invulnerable to erosion from 'subversives'. This is not to imply that no change was happening, but that the ruling élite considered itself secure at that time, the monarchies appeared still to be strong in certain nations, social attitudes and divisions were clearly defined, and expansion plus exploitation of foreign lands held the key to economic expansion at little cost. The star of the British Empire was at its apex and many thought that (relatively) all was well with the world.

The shadow of the opposition began to lengthen, disturbing the calm and the status quo, and suspicions began to deepen regarding the early stirrings of new developments in new thinking – culturally, politically and socially. Whilst these would still take several years to burst into open public view, this was their gestation period, prior to the crises of World War, Russian Revolution and economic collapse, etc.

The rumblings of the underground reshaping of the world began to be heard by some on on the surface, who felt as if they were sitting on the peak of an extinct volcano, believing it to be safe. Occultism began to be more attractive to many in the West, reflecting the need for inner transmutation experienced by people, and several major occult personalities who were to emerge into greater attention during the early 1920s (the period of the trine), such as Alice Bailey, Rudolf Steiner and Gurdjieff were undergoing their earlier phases of experience, training and initiation at this time. Of interest is the release in April 1904 of *The Book of the Law* through Aleister Crowley in the Cairo workings, in which the 'Word of the New Aeon' was transmitted into world consciousness. The closeness of this occult announcement and the opposition aspect to sound the death-knell of the old order and the birth of the new, is quite suggestive.

The changes triggered at this time, the commencement of a new century, and the last in this millennium, are still reverberating today, many of them still unresolved or transferred to different exponents of national conflicts. There is still the need for more people capable of thinking for themselves, to be less dependent upon relying upon others to make decisions for them, to lessen the power of individuals of influence and to share power and responsibility for the state of society amongst its members.

The influence of the Uranian ideals was opposed by the need for an emotionally biased sense of security represented by the familiar and traditional ways; the clash between them bringing world disruption. The influence of Pluto was initially used to give support to the old ways, but is correctly received as a means of subverting the Establishment, so that the new can be born, a process that we are still experiencing.

RETROGRADE URANUS

With the retrograde Uranus, the inner emphasis is firmly placed on the theme of freedom. This need, desire and demand is a central motivating factor in making personal decisions and choices. At times, due to the demands of society and individual family obligations, there may be severe conflict experienced through the agitation and pull of this powerful urge to be free. Whilst the clash between the old and the new will be felt, there will be no real peace until the surrender to the new paths has been made. Resistance to this impulse will create inner stress and tension, and ultimately will collapse in failure, as the potentially creative intent of Uranus displays its quality of shattering the structures of a life in which it is being denied free access.

The persona of the 'inner rebel' will be to the forefront of consciousness, aching to break any restraining ties and social traditions that are believed to be inhibiting its destined right of freedom. The personal feeling is one of discontent, restlessness and searching for this utopian state of 'freedom' for the self and for society. There is a strong sense of empathy with the desires, needs and hopes of the collective, and a belief that, in some way, this personal struggle to become free and to discover a fulfilling self-expression is of value not just for the self but for everyone.

There is likely to be a feeling of social responsibility; libertarian ideals are held, and social concepts related to 'liberty, equality and fraternity' are believed in. There is a futuristic optimism, and the individual with this retrograde Uranus can serve as a seed for future developments of humanity, through acting as a channel seeding and releasing those advanced ideas that will eventually flower as the future of humanity. These ideas can appear to be strange, impractical, crazy or naïve to others, and may in fact be incapable of being manifested in the present world. Yet the world has been built from people's dreams and hopes, and as it is certain thát the future will be built on the platform of contemporary dreams, so it is perhaps wiser to dream the highest idealistic dreams possible, in the belief that mankind can one day embody them to a satisfactory degree. A holistic, visionary perspective can reveal a way for man to travel in accord with the destined evolutionary pattern of unfoldment.

This world struggle for slow progress is unending, yet it will be felt as if it is a personal crusade, and that it is essential that the individual can make a vital difference. This can create an inner pressure to 'change the world', and a modification to a personal understanding of this feeling is probably necessary to gain a right perspective. What this involves is being true to one's own beliefs and personal path, expressing those innate gifts and talents to the maximum degree possible, and being willing to share any insights with others and so light their personal fire from the fire of your own inner torch. Over time, the light of the individual fires will spread and illuminate the way for all to see.

Personal relationships can prove difficult, especially if these inner conflicts cause friction between heart and mind, when there are obstacles facing any forward progress, like social and family commitments. An inner loneliness can be experienced, but a clear alignment to the function of seed-bearer can help to alleviate any personal reactions, through an association with the overshadowing group consciousness. Others may fail to understand you properly, and you may have to resist that temptation to brush aside any who you feel are standing in your way, perhaps through trying to make you conform to a socially acceptable lifestyle.

URANUS EXALTED IN SCORPIO

This is the key to that peculiar quality within the Uranus vibration that is reminiscent of the theme of death and rebirth to be found with Scorpio associations. It is in the sign of Scorpio that the purest, most transformative essence of the Uranus energy is released, emphasising that element of destructiveness that can characterise these two energies. This is also the link between the transpersonal functions of Uranus and Pluto (as ruler of Scorpio), and that esoteric connection between Uranus the Hierophant, and Pluto ruler of the group of spiritual disciples. It is as the Hierophant of the Sacred Mysteries that Uranus touches the 'group disciple' with the rod or wand of initiation, transmitting that electrical fire and so stimulating the process of initiation and transformation. This is a process which closes one cycle of existence and ushers in the new phase, and so fulfils that purpose of both Uranus and Pluto of a re-creation through revolutionary and evolutionary progression.

Uranus thus starts this process, preparing the ground for the work of Pluto to undermine all outlived structures within the individual, organisation or State, combining in a suitable way to aid in the creation of a better foundation for the new vision. It is from Uranus that the new idea, ideal or symbolic image initially emerges (thus reflecting that concept of Divine Ideation), and begins to stimulate the changes needed to embody the new pattern through revolutionary agitation in whichever sphere of life is to be transformed. Pluto then takes up the mantle of formulating this in a way that allows for the process of manifestation to occur on the physical plane. Uranus as the Sky God, and Air element co-operates with Pluto as the more earthing God of the Underworld to make this vision appear in the mediating realm of Gaia.

NATAL CHARTS

Two major aspects of the characteristics of Uranus involve the political and creative dimensions of life, where new visions are transmitted through the individual for collective absorption, and are designed to revolutionise mental attitudes and perception. To consider these operating through the lives of historically famous people, I have chosen three political figures of considerable stature: John F. Kennedy, Mahatma Gandhi and Sir Winston Churchill; a musician, John Lennon; and a notorious occultist, Aleister Crowley. These natal charts are viewed through the perspective of the Uranus influence on their lives and personal expressions, so that the transpersonal effect can stand out in stark relief, showing how essentially they became archetypal transmitters of 'visions from beyond', and how also, in three cases, they reflected sacrificial myths.

Aleister Crowley

Aleister Crowley was born in 1875, and died in 1947, and has been dubbed by the media 'the most wicked man on earth', which is an exaggeration in a period which also produced men like Stalin and Hitler. He has a reputation of being a 'black magician', yet anyone who has seriously studied his writings will know that his aspiration was towards the very highest spiritual ideals. For all his personality faults and contradictions, he was – on a transpersonal level – a 'holy illuminated man of God'. Often we consider God to be ineffable and incomprehensible, yet still judge his messengers according to pre-formed ideas of 'godliness' which preclude seeing any spark of the unique personalities that they are. Crowley was very complex, very intelligent and a joker. His irreverence would get him into trouble, as would his iconoclastic desire to discover truth. Israel Regardie's *Eye of the Triangle* is the most informed and revealing study of Crowley and his work.

Crowley had Uranus sextile Sun, square Mercury, sextile Venus, opposition Saturn and square Pluto. Uranus is in Leo, in the 1st house. His Sun is Libra, with Leo Ascendant.

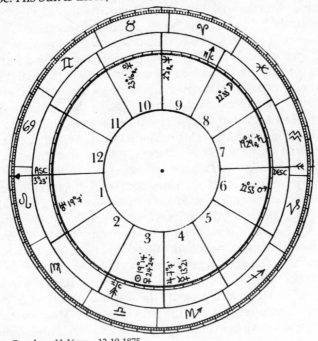

Aleister Crowley 11.16pm   12.10.1875
Leamington Spa, England

A Libran Sun is usually like a swinging pendulum, moving between polarised extremes, finding difficulty in settling into a balanced position and displaying a changeable temperament. The influence of Uranus pours through its natal position in Leo, in the 1st house. This implies a need to redefine the personal identity, and to exalt it to 'kingship', and is a motivation for self-exploration and to achieve a state of personal elevation. This is the sphere of Crowley's revolution. The route that he chose was the royal high path of 'magick' (as he spelled it), aiming to transform himself into 'Godhood', and nothing less would suffice. Initially, he was trained in the Hermetic Order of the Golden Dawn, but became involved in schisms and releasing secret information and eventually left to form his own magical orders.

The analysis of Uranus in the 1st house is very apt for the personality of Crowley. What is remarkable is the sheer will and determination that he applied in moving beyond the conscious persona, and through a lifetime of exploring his psyche with magical and yogic techniques. He was a precursor of the current 'New Age' approach and contemporary magical techniques are often based on those of the Golden Dawn. In Crowley's own eyes, he became the Logos of the New Age, pronouncing his Uranian message in 'Thelema': 'Do what thou wilt shall be the whole of the Law. Love under Will.' This is the most misunderstood formula, which actually involves a transformation in the individual prior to their being capable of discovering their own true will (or Self).

Crowley was both a reactionary against the staidness of his society, and a revolutionary fervently proclaiming his world message like a new messiah. He demanded total freedom for himself, considered all forms of self-discovery to be acceptable, hugely enjoyed breaking social taboos, and so became socially dangerous. Crowley's influence was often 'destructive' in effect (not in nature), mainly because of the effect it had on people who had difficulty in handling it correctly. Often Crowley had problems absorbing the energies flowing through his opened mind. He had a vision in which everyone was in tune with their higher self, creating a society of conscious freedom, where each was following their own truth without clashing with others, essentially one of diversity in unity.

He offered the path of magic as the way to achieve this, reflecting the Sun–Uranus sextile, and the struggles of the Mercury–Uranus square show his inner conflicts. Much of Crowley's life is summed up by the Saturn–Uranus opposition, and the effort to transcend these dualistic opposites. In him, the past and future fused; he stood at the intersection from which he transmitted the 'New World of the Aeon' and unfolded his Book of the Law. He was a culmination of past magical and radical social traditions, and the prophet of the liberation of the new. Breaking free of Saturnian boundaries, he embodied a unique display in Uranian characteristics, both positive and negative.

In today's blasé world, he would not be so unique; but he could be said to be one of the openers of the door, a man before his time, almost like a Renaissance man. Magician, poet, novelist, yogi, mountaineer, teacher and prophet. We are his heirs, in the sense that we too are asked to embody that spirit which operated through him.

John Lennon

John Lennon's music took him from the streets of Liverpool onto a world stage, and immortalised him as a contemporary hero of popular music through his involvement with the Beatles. Whilst the Beatles were popularisers of styles of black music, R 'n' B, and early rock and roll, somehow they became transformed into the leading figureheads of a new musical direction and mass youth movement in the early and mid sixties. They became the archetypal group, a source of inspiration for many following musicians, and their image was much purer than the actual reality of their lives. As a group, they struck keynotes that resonated with emerging social developments, musically and culturally, and they associated with the avant-garde of the time. From drug experimentation to meditation, and in Lennon's case to radical politics, they helped to give voice to the searching of the young for new values, attitudes and ways of living.

From his early youth, Lennon was a leather-jacketed rebel, anti-authoritarian, anti-leaders, iconoclastic and irreverent. Underlying this was a sometimes fragmented personality, defensively belligerent, one which contained raging emotional conflicts, which are indicated in the Venus–Uranus square. In trying to come to understand his emotions, he explored methods such as Primal Therapy, and tried to give voice to his anguish through his lyrics. That square aspect also shows a restless nature, moving through periodic changes, and driven by an urge to explore new experiences. Many of the inner tensions were released through the channel of music, as Lennon began to use the creative energies of the trines of Uranus to the Moon and Mars. To many, Lennon was a harbinger of a socially dangerous message, and they felt that his rhythmic music, his lyrics ('I'd love to turn you on . . .') and his iconoclastic statements – such as that the Beatles were now more popular and relevant than Jesus – were subversive to contemporary youth. Problems with governmental authorities over visas in the States were linked to his association with political radicals and his anti-war songs and státements of the Vietnam era. To the Establishment, he was a thorn in their side, embodying a free and questioning attitude that they did not wish to encourage. With the Beatles, he wrote the song of the sixties vision, 'All You Need is Love' which was transmitted on a world-wide satellite link-up, and in his solo career moved towards songs of clear social and political comment, like 'Power to the People' and 'Imagine'. These songs represent Uranian ideals, and the messages of social revolution, in a time when belief in the power of music to change the world was still strong.

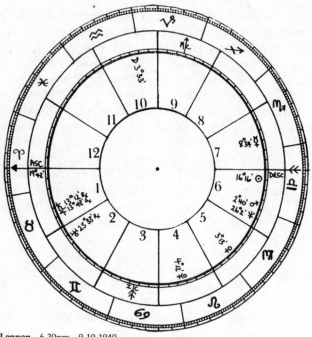

John Lennon 6.30pm 9.10.1940
Liverpool, England

Much of his personal confusion came from the conflict between his awareness of his own complex and not always pleasant nature, and the idealistic themes that he felt he had to express through his music. The time of Lennon's birth is given by Hunter Davies as 6.30 p.m., and if that is accurate, it gives an Aries Ascendant and Libra Sun, with Uranus in the 2nd house in Taurus. If this is so, then we can see Lennon's progress to fame and fortune still leaving him feeling empty.

He had succeeded in making use of natural talents and re-sources, but was confronted with the issues of meaning and values at the peak of material success. New dimensions of life were shared with him by Yoko Ono, political and cultural aspects came to the fore, and by the time of his assassination, he had begun to feel more at peace with himself and his life, as he entered middle age and had integrated his emotional challenges more effectively. At the time of his death, transiting Uranus was in Scorpio in his 8th house; during a personal phase of rebirth and enjoyment of the family, he was murdered.

Winston Churchill

Sir Winston Churchill became identified with the British bulldog spirit during World War II, and was an embodiment of those national characteristics which were essential in opposing Nazi Germany. Churchill had Uranus trine Sun and Venus, square Mercury and Pluto, sextile Mars, and opposition Saturn. Uranus was placed in the 11th house, in Leo.

The Uranus–Pluto square is interesting, in that it was made in 1931–34 during the time of Hitler's grasping of power, prior to the World War. Churchill was born under the influence of the square in 1874, and intuitively recognised the dangers of separatist national attitudes which were emerging through Germany and Hitler as focused through their demagogues and dictators. He warned the British Government of the dangers of a resurrected Germany, and advised a new build-up of armaments to resist the war that he felt sure would come.

Churchill's political career was varied, with several changes of party allegiance and changes of mind connected to his need to retain his independence of thought and attitude. Sometimes he was in favour with the party establishments of Liberals and Conservatives, other times he almost became a persona non grata. Through his assertion of personal freedom, he never became a reliable 'party man', and his political career had several peaks and troughs before he headed the coalition government of the war years. The Mars sextile and Venus and Sun trines indicate some of his social and creative characteristics. Apart from being a politician, he was also a lecturer, historian and artist of ability. The Mercury square indicates his obstinacy and rebelliousness, which he never attempted to hide, yet which often forced him into stances of political alienation and into the 'wilderness'.

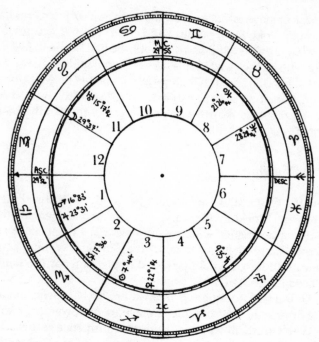

Winston Churchill 1.30am 30.11.1874
Blenheim Palace, Oxfordshire, England

Yet he was the right man to lead his country in a time of need. An archetype of the British race was transmitted through his characteristics; the Uranian ideal of freedom became the flag linking the allies against the imposition of the Axis forces of Germany, Italy and Japan. His famous speeches, designed to galvanise the will of the people against the enemy, stimulated the desires for freedoms which were under threat, as well as supporting the martian energies. Churchill acted as a medium for the British will, amplified by his role as national leader, as noted in Uranus placed in Leo, he became a king-like figure in all but name. This echoes the role of the legendary Arthur as 'Dux Bellorum' or Warlord, fighting against the threat of national invasion by the enemy. With Uranus in the 11th house, it is a group consciousness that operates through him 'in alliance with others, you can determine your social role, which is to give a collective voice, as the whole speaks through a unified group consciousness'. In effect, he succeeded in helping protect the emerging world Uranian vision from those who would destroy it. Yet, shortly after the time of his greatest triumph and the defeat of

Hitler, he was rejected by the people, who preferred the new Labour vision of a reconstructed society. As in the ancient myth of the sacrificial king, where the old king was periodically ritually deposed in order to generate new life and fertility, Churchill's time had passed. He had fulfilled his transpersonal function as a protector of the light. It is slightly ironic that a man who had lived as independently as possible in his career, had suffered for his views, eventually ended up as a focal point for a group spirit, transmitting its message to its people.

John F. Kennedy

In many ways, John F. Kennedy has become mythologised by the American people since the time of his assassination, and almost symbolises the young king cut down in his prime as another sacrificial victim of the idealistic dream that they were attempting to externalise. Obviously, the reality of Kennedy and his political career is much more down to earth than the light in which many now perceive him, and the glitter of his political 'Camelot' is tarnished, yet the glamour of the people's aspiration and high ideals still are associated with him. This reflects the nature of the high Uranian vision; despite its descent into the depths of human life, and the distortions that it undergoes in this process and its apparent failure to be achieved in human society, the quality of its light remains pure and untouched. It is an assertion that the ideal stimulating the French, American and Russian revolutions is perpetually unscathed, and that it is us that have to live up to the divine dream.

Under the influence of his father, Joseph Kennedy, and the dynastic nature of his wealthy family, the lives of John and his brothers were expected to develop along a track laid out by his father. They were prepared to become influential social leaders. In the Uranus–Mercury square aspect, we can see the struggle of Kennedy to rebel against the parental will. Yet the mixture of parental design and his own adult desire for power would lead him in that fated life direction. His attempts at rebellion were always constrained by circumstances, and could only be allowed expression through certain channels. This meant that eventually, the rebel developed policies for radical social change, which were genuinely believed would offer the potential to improve the quality of American life. Such policies would attract opposition. Kennedy develop'ed a political image and formula to express necessary social changes, a style of vision that has proved more attractive after his death than during his own term of presidential office.

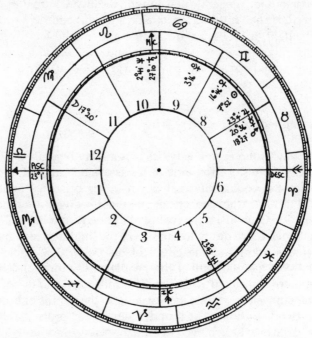

John F. Kennedy 3.15pm   29.5.1917
Brookline, Mass., USA

Several of his personal challenges are reflected in the Uranus–Jupiter square; in an effort to resolve certain inner pressures and to express a political consistency, he relied greatly upon an intimate group of close advisors, who forged his policies into a resemblance of cohesiveness and clarity. Kennedy often had difficulty in being clear what he wanted to do; often – with his agreement - he became the spokesman for the supporting group. Like the Uranus–Mars square, he wavered between moving fearlessly into the new, and staying with the old; each foot straddling across the divide on opposite sides. This is the usual political compromise, radical speeches but a slower movement towards actual implementation due to public reaction. A Gemini Sun and Libra Ascendant offers a mental focus, but can work against stable, decisive thinking.

There was some emotional repression, which is common in

mány social leaders and politicians, where feelings had to be controlled in order to view political decisions dispassionately. His relationships were often lacking in depth, and often there was considerable distancing from his wife, who some believe had been married for her social standing and to add to the glamour of the young politician. His affairs and sexual conquests were apparently numerous, primarily focused on the physical level only. He lacked discretion in these, and they were covered up by his close associates, and in this sphere we can see his rebellious spirit being released in his insistence on acting in this way. His Uranus in the 5th house was exploring new love affairs, as an attempt to release the pressures that he felt. At the time of his death, transiting Uranus was in his 11th house, and a voice of the group consciousness was silenced.

It is the transpersonal dimension of Kennedy that still remains to be admired by people; he enunciated dreams and aspirations of the people, and had a charismatic aura. Ideas which emanate from a Uranian source often have an archetypal myth hidden deep within, and these can be expressed in logical and rational terms to people, thus communicating them. To some degree, Kennedy achieved this, and in so doing transmits the associated myth of King Arthur and his court of Camelot, becoming an 'undying king' who will one day be resurrected again when the need is there. Many people in America still refuse to believe that Kennedy is dead; in an archetypal sense, that is true, because his inspiration will work through other channels in its attempt to communicate its eternal vision.

Mahatma Gandhi

Similar to Churchill and Kennedy, Mohandas Gandhi became identified as an embodiment of a transpersonal vision. He became known as 'Mahatma', meaning great soul, for his life-long efforts to achieve freedom and liberation from oppression for his people. He was a lawyer in Africa before he embarked on his crusade for racial equality, and he was inspired by the energies pouring through his Uranus–Pluto sextile which led him onto the public stage as a reformer and social revolutionary. This aspect, as I commented earlier, invokes a natural voice of the people to speak out against social injustice and hypocrisy, to resist dictatorial abuse of power and influence emanating from central government, and to insist upon a high quality of governmental leadership, ideals and morality. The Uranus–Neptune square he succeeded in resolving, so that his revolutionary tendencies began to be communicated through a consistent belief structure and philosophy of non-violence. It was this philosophy of non-violent resistance to oppression that began to inspire his followers, and yet was also a reawakening of earlier Indian religious teachings, being transmitted through another Uranian channel into the world.

The Venus–Uranus trine reveals personal values founded on a world social perspective. With this aspect the ideal is to live in a way that both satisfies personal needs and has a beneficial effect upon the wider world. Gandhi had very powerful personal principles and disciplines which he lived up to, which impressed his supporters who attempted to follow his path. In the times of civil unrest between the Hindus and Muslims, he entered situations where he was prepared to lose his life if necessary in order to confront the antagonists with his non-violent philosophy. Through the power of his convictions, he overcame severe obstacles on his political path. The Mars–Uranus trine indicates the rebellious spirit who becomes an opponent of the Establishment, yet attempts to change society

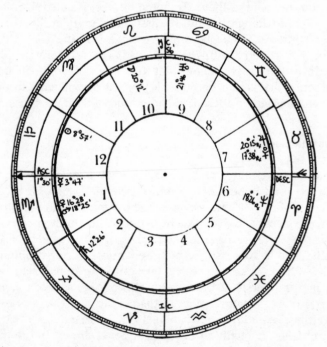

Mohandas Gandhi   7.33am   2.10.1869
Porbandar, India

from within as a spokesman for a minority or disadvantaged social group.

Gandhi became a servant of India; many perceive him as the archetypal image of the Founding Father of modern India, free from the oppression of colonial rule, as a result of his efforts to gain Indian independence. Here we note again the Uranian characteristics of freedom and liberation. The Jupiter–Uranus sextile indicates an approach that builds the future on the foundations of the past, through the mediating influence of the present, which is what Gandhi did with his spiritually based philosophy. Applying this sextile and his Uranus placed in the 9th house of the higher mind, he became a teacher whose insights and positive optimistic attitudes helped to communicate the potential of a brighter future to others. He believed that there were answers to be found for everything and that all obstacles could be overcome. Gandhi was also to be assassinated as a result of his social and transpersonal vision of human unity and peaceful living; the transmitting of the energy of change stimulates an equal and opposite reaction of resistance. In the struggle between the two, we can slowly make progress, inch by inch.

The Chart of the USSR

The 'natal chart' of the Union of Soviet Socialist Republics is an interesting case to study in respect of the influence of Uranus upon a national state. This has been calculated from the period of the Russian Revolution, and marks the distinct 'birth' of the USSR as a new entity in the world. What the chart can reflect is the overshadowing pattern inherent in the idea of the USSR which helped to create the revolution, and which is the conditioning pattern behind the world expression of the USSR today. Similar to the previous American and French revolutions, the driving urge was to overthrow the monarchial domination of the Tsars and nobility, and to establish a free people's republic and to enter 'a new world'.

National revolutions tend to occur when there is a synchronicity of a powerful yet detached and unsympathetic ruling élite, and the arising within the collective of an idea or vision that is being projected as a viable alternative and more appealing image of living. Usually, the people and their spokesmen feel oppressed by the decisions of the ruling élite, and may consider them to be dissipated, degenerate and certainly unfit to rule. It is the emergence of a vision of a new society, which embodies an archetypal energy, power and resonance that begins to attract support and galvanises the people to agitate for change. This again reflects the antagonistic polarity between the status quo and traditional, established ways of Saturn, and the urge to change and shatter of Uranus.

In the case of Tsarist Russia, it was the concepts of Communism and Marxism that were the focus for this collective archetypal dream and desire. The liberation of an oppressed people to create their own people's republic operating under the ideal of Communism was the intent. This was the 'ideal vision of the future' stimulated by Uranus that generated the power in the people to bring down the Tsarist régime.

As is often the case, it turned into a violent and bloody revolution, with conflicting group power struggles attempting to take control in rapidly intensifying chaotic circumstances. It is this apparently destructive element of Uranian change that becomes immediately recognisable; perhaps it is inevitable when opposed by a resistant entrenched status quo. But the power of an unleashed Uranian vibration through the collective unconscious cannot be denied, especially by a crystallised Establishment structure. Under the social pressures and the success of Lenin and the Bolshevik political grouping, the State machinery of the Tsars collapsed and the shattering liberative effect of Uranus occurred, prior to the restorative quality of Saturn re-entering to re-establish the new structures, boundaries and collective lifestyle through the introduction of the Communist–Marxist philosophy into the new state.

There is some dispute concerning the date and time of the birth of the USSR. This chart has been computer-calculated for 10.52 p.m. 7 November 1917, Leningrad.

A study of the chart to evaluate the Uranian influence can be quite suggestive, as it embodies several major factors associated with this planet.

Uranus is placed in Aquarius, thus emphasising that vibration, and indicating an affinity with the mind and the element of air. This implies that the Uranian vision will be highly idealised, futuristic and probably too advanced to be easily assimilated and integrated into that society. It is always a goal to be aimed towards, similar to the developing results of both the American and French revolutions, where neither state has succeeded in actualising their founding ideals.

Uranus in this chart is placed in the 7th house of social relationships. Whilst an important theme of Marxism is that of the power

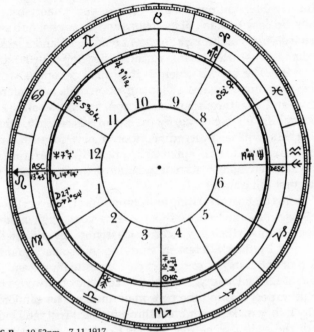

U.S.S.R. 10.52pm 7.11.1917
Leningrad

of the working class through equality, co-operation and power-sharing within the overall economic philosophy, which could be reflected through Uranus–Aquarius in the 6th house, I think that such an association ties down the thrust of the Uranus vision into a materialistic cul-de-sac. It is certainly a strong element in the contemporary expression of the USSR, yet Uranus does not like to become too identified with the world of Gaia. A 7th house placing would reflect the function of relationship that Uranus is challenged with, and that need to relate spirit and matter.

Many of the modern problems that the USSR faces are associated with the spheres of relationships, internally and externally. It is a grouping of republic states under a central co-ordinating bureaucracy, which has a variety of racial types and social and religious groupings to integrate and unite. It is an extremely large state, with problems of communication, culture and economics. It has an ambiguous relationship with the external international world, with its client-satellite states, relationships with states on its national boundaries, and an antagonistic mistrust of America and its European allies based on ideological differences. It is extremely sensitive to international criticism of its internal actions against dissidents and its interventions in other states, yet cannot seem to balance its ideals with many of its actions and decisions. As a state it is often insecure, exhibiting adolescent tendencies and a lack of social judgement as to the reactions of its relationship with the other world nations. The basic problem is that it has become a world power before completing more than a fraction of its own internal revolution, and thus through inner friction, frustration and pressure finds it difficult to change. By the end of this century, I think that the USSR will be proceeding upon a new form of inner revolution to complete its original task, especially as the transiting Uranus will be returning to its natal position of the 7th house at the end of its first full transit cycle.

The Uranus themes of relating and communication are reflected by the Soviet scientific and industrial emphasis upon modern technology, through their advanced space technology and satellite systems, and by their interest in studying inner space and the operation of the mind, through psychic investigations, and the exploring of ESP, telepathy, and electromagnetic brainwaves.

I would expect this to become a major interest for the USSR, especially if they make major breakthroughs, as it will satisfy that sphere of the state psyche that wishes to soar in the skies and become free. Exploring the realms of psychokinetic energy and quantum mechanics will eventually lead to the Uranian areas of imagination and creative visualisation, the 'thought creation', and it will be in this area that the USSR will find a new focus, satisfying that Uranian need to relate spirit and matter together. Currently, the balance in the USSR is too biased towards the materialistic perception, but this will change. Part of the impulse of enhanced technological progress is to apply the mind and intellect to sequentially liberate us from the confines and limitations of matter and physical bodies, so that we become more free from the domination of nature-Gaia. In fact, the first step to discover the real freedom lies in right relationship with Gaia and our physical nature and environment.

Part of the challenge now faced by the USSR is rooted in the Stalin years, when materialism was over-emphasised, and the cult of the dominating State father-figure emerged through the dictatorial role played by Stalin. This was more like a rebirth of the Saturn tendencies, where a strong earthing energy was paramount (as reflected by Stalin's Sun in Capricorn), and the temporary result was a binding of the higher aspects of the Uranian revolutionary vision. Modern USSR is starting to throw off these consciousness shackles once again, and the imminent unfoldment of mind and intellect towards realms beyond logic and rationality is starting. A reorientation towards the perception of the power of mind is happening. Initially it was seen as a power to enable mankind to master the environment; now it is changing from a less selfish exploitative approach to one of learning how best to co-operate with natural cycles and processes, so that the mind begins to harmonise with its environment instead of attempting to challenge it for supremacy.

The chart of the USSR displays a Scorpio Sun and a Leo Ascendant. This indicates the tendency for regeneration, rebirth and an affinity with the collective unconscious and the realm of Pluto via Scorpio. It is worth remembering that Uranus is exalted in Scorpio, and so that vibration will naturally affect the expression of the national purpose and destiny. Like America, the USSR is a cultural melting-pot of mixed races, and can symbolise a world need for integration and greater unity through its efforts to weld races and cultures into a cohesive whole. To the degree that it can do this successfully, it can indicate a potentially successful way for other world areas to follow. The Leo Ascendant reflects the urge for individuality and kingship, which we see in its worldwide expanpansionist policies, and in its inner struggle between the rights and freedoms of the individual and the dictates and demands of the State machinery. Obviously, a major part of the Leo energy is being repressed at present, but as Uranus is associated with the collective group objectives of the 11th house and its concepts of universalbrotherhood, the challenge is to liberate this individualist energy in such a way that it creates a group consciousness, and not enter a direct conflict with the power of the State. It is interesting to note Pluto's position in the 11th house, which reveals a wound and conflict, a challenge which will have to be resolved and a rebirth achieved in that sphere of life. This also parallels the world challenge facing us as we struggle to move into the Aquarian Age, which is essentially the same conflict, and one to which the role of the USSR is extremely important.

There are several main aspects of Uranus in this chart, all to planets placed in either Water or Fire signs. Uranus squares the Sun, which implies that an inner struggle of self-transformation is necessary. In order to release innate tensions, change, adaptation or mutation has to occur so that the way can be made clear to pursue the individual life direction and purpose, moving from an identification of Scorpio the scorpion to Scorpio the eagle, and from the materialistic earth to the freedom of the skies.

Uranus opposes the Moon in Leo, and here is the clash with the past and the Tsarist rulership under the desire for individual rights and freedom. It is a rejection and denial of the past traditions and roots, and of the Great Mother, where there can be a repression of all associated feeling and emotional values – a lack of heart – under the domination of a masculine Air principle. This struggle is also reflected through the opposition with Saturn, where the compulsive issue relates to the interplay between the individual and the State, and the degree to which personal freedoms can be allowed within the State framework, and where libertarian Uranian values could possibly erode the established pattern of the Saturnian social structures. The square with Mercury indicates some difficulty in communication, perhaps an eccentricity and ambiguity of decision and choice, where the Scorpio Sun-Uranus square creates a paranoid attitude which often determines the nature of choices made. This can be seen in the creation of protective boundary satellite states, repression of internal dissidence, and a defensive belligerency to Western states. Essentially, it is a fear of losing control.

The opposition with the Leo Ascendant should be perceived in the higher context of 'group consciousness', which is an Aquarian Age concept related to unity within diversity, and synergy, where the expression and power of the whole is greater than the sum of its parts. Both Uranus and Leo assert the value of unique individuality, but this clash is about the issue of self-unfoldment within the evolutionary progression of the associated group or state. The concepts of Communism and collective power where people work together for mutual benefits will be re-perceived and applied in a more effective manner.

Many of the emerging concepts of the Aquarian Age can be seen to involve a new form of merging between the ideals of democracy and Communism, and a right relationship emerging between the materialistic and spiritual impulses. The USSR will have a key role in this process.

CHAPTER 5

Uranus in the Natal Houses

THE NATAL HOUSE POSITION of Uranus will reveal the sphere of the individual life experience in which the characteristics of Uranus are most active. The specific house will be the doorway through which the transpersonal function of Uranus will be transmitted as a process of periodic changes, and in some cases, a confrontation with their individual 'destiny', if the person has a role to perform as a human channel for the Uranus message.

The natal house can indicate a point where sudden and unusual experiences can enter the life, those which bring permanent change in their wake. These can be both 'positive or negative' changes, depending upon what the individual is 'attracting' to themselves; opportunities can be presented, or shocking experiences can suddenly devastate the emotions. Yet even in the midst of pain and suffering, something positive can be discovered which may reorientate the remainder of the life.

The house is the sphere of life where the individual will most easily demonstrate the Uranus energy, both positive and negative tendencies. It is an energy which is capable of being drawn through to stimulate and awaken latent talents. Often, it is in that area of life that deep and long-lasting personal changes are experienced, and where that inner urge for renewal and transformation is most felt. Much depends on the nature and capacity of the person regarding their ability to change; Uranus will never stimulate more than the person is able to integrate, so there can be a level of uncertainty as to how profound a change Uranus can bring about in a person.

For the individual, the house will reflect aspects of the life where there is the strongest impulse to be unique and free. For instance, a 9th house position will imply a revolution on mental levels, through the intellect and a religious/philosophical outlook. Probably there will be a reaction against social traditions, and a need to discover a world-view that is unique and apt for that person. In whichever house Uranus is placed, there will be a pull towards breaking and defying the status quo and convention. Also, the nature of the house will indicate the type of friends that will be preferred, and the type of social groups that the individual will be eventually associated with through 'natural gravitation' of like minds.

URANUS IN THE 1ST HOUSE

The 1st house is the sphere of self-discovery and the expression of that unique individuality. As the commencement of this house is the point of the Ascendant, it symbolises the birth of the new person and the remainder of the 'house wheel' covers the areas of daily living that will be explored and expressed over the course of the lifetime.

Uranus in this position will tend to be disruptive in the attempt to form a relatively stable personality, and for anyone with this placing, it will be an ongoing challenge to feel inwardly at ease with their own nature, due to that sense of flux and mutability.

What is probably required is a new perception and relationship with the inner self beyond the ever-changeable personality. It should be clearly understood that the personality is a mask and façade for social living, and that its very nature is multi-faceted and variable. One should not identify with that persona, and a degree of detachment from the superficial levels of mind and emotions and body may need to be made, so that a deeper point of stability can be found within the self. There are many techniques to achieve this new integration, and one that can be usefully performed is the exercise of dis-identification used in psychosynthesis.

Uranus will stimulate you to be highly 'unique', eccentric and erratic, possibly feeling forced into performing so that the impression of difference is conveyed to an audience. If left alone, you are likely to experience some inner difficulty and unease, feeling that there is no stable or permanent centre. To avoid this, you may generate a whirl of outer superficial activity, so that you can perceive yourself and infer a 'centre' through the mirroring of other people's reactions; also, it diminishes the time available to become self-preoccupied and to experience this sense of lack.

A revolution of identity is required by Uranus. This message may be conveyed to you through a variety of sources; there may be sudden surprise shocks which awaken personal insights and realisations; opportunities may be offered 'out of the blue', especially those which could take you to new environments and create the possibility to recreate your individuality with unknown people, shaking you out of habit patterns of behaviour; there may be drastic, life-changing experiences, which offer temporary chaos which forces changes upon you. Uranus will periodically 'prod you' into response, trying to redirect you towards that transformation.

Freedom and a need for unconventional living will be motivating factors, and will work against you settling for a staid, routine-bound lifestyle. Change and variety excite you, and with that restless spirit your life will have many alterations in attitudes, directions, beliefs, relationships. Caught up in your own needs and often selfish tendencies, you can act with a lack of sensitivity and concern for others, and that obstinate streak in you can create friction with intimate partners.

Your personality can confuse and frustrate others. It has a mutability and quicksilver style at times which amplified by that urge for newness can add an element of inconsistency and unreliability. This may need to be consciously moderated, especially as you are likely to feel attracted towards involvements with futuristic alternative groups, where you may aspire towards leadership positions. If you have succeeded in finding a deeper centre beyond the superficial personality, then directing your energies into these channels could be ideal.

The challenge facing you is to allow the Uranian energy to transform that understanding and sense of self. It involves a search to discover what you are, who you are, and then to assert your uniqueness. An unconscious reaction to these needs will revolve around that fragile superficial personality, the 'actor' self, and a deeper integration is what is really required to embody the new life creativity of Uranus.

URANUS IN THE 2ND HOUSE

The issues confronted here are those of resources, possessions and values. Uranus requires changes to be made in these spheres of life, and will influence you to achieve the necessary adjustments.

As you develop in life, you will naturally acquire possessions, unfold personal talents and gifts, and build a set of personal values which act as a guide to directions chosen and decisions made. It is a question of meaning and inner relationship to 'material substance' that is important. Often, social attitudes are unconsciously acquired through childhood programming, perhaps those of your parents, or of the wider community. These can develop in various ways. There may be a family lack of material possessions, a desire to become rich and to be able to indulge in materialistic prosperity; values and meaning could have been imposed, through pressures placed on the child to succeed at school and to elevate the family status by achieving a university degree; meaning could have been placed in frugality and lack of waste; importance could have been put into unfolding personal talents, or conversely, these could have been denied or frustrated by family circumstances, like the little girl pianist who had to cease lessons because the family could not afford the tuition. This 'programming' can accumulate in many ways, some positive and some negative in impact.

By the time of adulthood, many attitudes are fixed in the psyche, and adult needs of becoming independent and starting their own homes and family also contribute to inner choices, frustration and desires. An over-reliance and dependence on material possessions for that sense of identity and status can develop. A preoccupation with achieving material success and prosperity can dominate a life to the exclusion of other interests. A turning away from ostentatious wealth can occur in those born into such circumstances, who reject the 'family inheritance' (at least whilst they are young and idealistic . . .).

Each one of us has some patterns operating within which dominate our attitudes, choices and value structures. This position of Uranus is questioning such assumed patterns, suggesting that a little revolution is required here. You may need to unblock the channels which inhibit innate creative gifts and talents, which so far you have failed to externalise, perhaps through a lack of confidence, determination or opportunity. Evaluate your skills and potential talents, list all those assets that are yours to exploit; potentially, they could change your life, liberate you from an unsuitable situation. Most people are sadly under-used, deadening themselves in undemanding jobs, and limiting their options in life. You may need to wake up, look closely at those personal resources and material possessions and consider how they could be used more wisely and effectively, especially if you are discontented with certain aspects of your life. What are your values in life? Do you even know what they are? Write down what is really important to you, and what you would really like to do in your life. Are these what you are actually doing? Probably not . . . but there may be a way to achieve them if certain changes were made. Often we settle for convenience, second best, plod along well-worn grooves, dreaming of what we would prefer! Uranus says 'Change, and try to make that dream real!' We are only sure of having one life – irrespective of the reincarnation theory – and generally society encourages us to virtually waste it, and we collaborate through passivity and fear. Is that what we really want? We postpone things into the future, saying 'Well, one day I'll do this, or do that, when I have the time . . .' Could we really live like that if we applied the truth of the saying 'How long is your life? As long as your next breath!' Following that could lead to extremist behaviour from unconscious minds, but certainly we could all greatly improve our lives if we so chose.

Uranus can bring financial wealth or poverty, depending upon the required lesson. You may find it easy to accumulate money, then in over-expanding, make a mistake and lose it all. The key is that inner programming. Resources, talents, possessions and personal values can make or break a life. Use yours wisely.

URANUS IN THE 3RD HOUSE

This involves the levels of mind and social communication, which has a certain affinity with Uranus, yet can be expressed with a less than unifying style, due to that eccentric unconventional quality.

It is mainly the lower level of mind – the separatist analytical aspect – that this house is related to, and there will be an emphasis on scientific perception, logic, rationality, impersonality. Uranus will add the attraction towards more unusual areas of investigation, and will increase the ability to think freely, which can often be lacking in analytical minds which dissect yet fail to see 'the wood for the trees'. The Uranian individuality will also resist obvious influencing by other minds, usually insisting upon its right to hold its unique opinions, which can often be much less unique than it prefers to believe.

Your nature will be exploratory in style, mentally and physically; curiosity will drive you, together with that need for new horizons and new ideas. At times, the speed of your intellect can lead to insights that border on intuition, but the degree of connective logic can be erratic and jumps are often made. Sometimes this can lead to forming impractical ideas and schemes, and your enthusiasm may make you overlook crucial factors in their formulation or omit important steps in carrying them out. Structuring such ideas is often a weak point, as you are primarily interested in the idea rather than the work needed to manifest it on the physical plane. Your mind will tend to be restless and changeable, always ready to rush onward towards the next 'bright idea' or information that is attracting your attention.

Reflecting the Uranus concerns, you will be attracted towards progressive revolutionary concepts in any area of interest (you will rarely interest yourself in studying the past, unless you need to develop foundational data). Eventually, these may be expressed through words, either written or spoken; active physical revolution is not to your taste. This brings you into association with like-minded groups and individuals, and can help to bring some focus into your life.

This 3rd house involves the application of intelligence in adapting to the environment, a fairly pragmatic approach, yet a necessary life skill. It is a 'learning to do', an ability to function adequately within the structures of that particular society, and implies a certain degree of restrictive specialisation to live in prescribed ways. Uranus will probably subvert this in a twofold way. First, a reorientation is required in the activity of the analytical mind; this is towards a more unifying structure of synthesis, of drawing together a multiplicity of fragments into a cohesive whole, creating a revelatory centre of wholeness which then reflects a totally new perception of life. This is the way of the future, and you can share in the task of making that dream a reality. The second is perhaps a lesser task, but still personally important. The task of improving your own adaptation and functioning in society, and in communication with others. This can require more self-discipline in focusing your mind, and directing that talent for making the best use of ideas. This is an anchoring within matter of ephemeral ideas and thoughts, making them tangible and capable of a practical application. All movement towards these dual aims would greatly help the revolution in this house.

URANUS IN THE 4TH HOUSE

With this placement, there will be a focus upon the themes of family, foundations and roots in life. It is likely that there was some type of disruption or unusual way of living during your childhood. This could have manifested in a variety of ways, which can have the effect of creating either instability or a more interesting and exciting childhood.

In the contemporary world, this can often take the form of parental marriage difficulties, family friction and divorce, where one of the parents eventually leaves the family home, and the children are plunged into a bewildering emotional situation where parental conflict and childhood emotional immaturity conspire to develop inner problems of adjustment. Even adults find such traumatic crises difficult to deal with; children often lock them away, sometimes festering into guilt associations, and blaming themselves for the breakdown of the adult relationship.

There may be frequent changes of residence, perhaps caused by parental choice or careers, which periodically uproot a child from a familiar environment and friends, forcing them to confront 'new unknown worlds' and so stand alone (if only temporarily), being forced to adapt quickly to new homes, schools and friends, even different countries. Such an early lifestyle can be either beneficial or damaging; much depends upon the age of the child, the support from parents, and the individual point of development and ability to deal with a changing environment. In several ways, it can speed the maturation process, with the child soon accepting responsibility and sensibly applying intelligence to its actions and choices, as well as offering a broader perception of the varieties and differences that life presents through experiencing different communities or countries. Yet it can also create a pattern of instability, a lack of roots, a need to modify 'self' without having an established centre to work from.

In some cases, home may be a social gathering place, less family-focused, but a place which parents use for meetings of common interests; political, religious, cultural, etc. This can have a positive aspect in meeting a wider variety of people, yet can also be 'negative' in that a lack of attention and interest from the busy parents can lead to a fragmentation of the relationship bonds. Perhaps too much freedom is given to such children, because the parents need the time for their own interests, and so the child develops without a necessary discipline and able to indulge in most of its desires; this could create future adult problems in coping with the responsibilities and obligations with which modern life confronts people.

Whatever the nature of the family roots, these will affect the psychological foundations of the developing individual, and eventually play an important role in the decision-making of the adult. Uranus is implying that a reorientation is required in respect of these acquired or inherited roots. There may be problems involved in the personal family relationship to a social, ethnic or economic background, a reaction to which dictates future choices, perhaps through attempting to escape or transcend them, or in proving that success can still be achieved despite such a background. It can be a highly motivating factor.

The issue is that of integration and stability, and the establishment of a firm psychological centre which can act as a focusing self, from which the adult life is consciously directed. This is the challenge represented by Uranus, where a new foundation is required in order for you to experience and enjoy life more fully. A sense of inner instability needs to be transformed into a deeper, more integrative centre, which is capable of uniquely expressing personal creativity, and operating in a positive manner.

URANUS IN THE 5TH HOUSE

This will involve the sudden movement outwards of 'emotionally based energy', where involvements with the external world, people and creative expressions will be the main sphere of activity.

Essentially this will be through the projection of emotionally rooted energy, and can involve spontaneous falling in love, inspired artistic creations and a search for pleasure, enjoyment, fun and excitement. A lack of self-discipline is likely, as you can easily submit to passing love affairs and the attractions of a carefree life. There may be an element of immaturity and childlike displays of behaviour at times. This is not necessarily 'bad', but they are often expressed at inopportune times; others may demand that you grow up.

It can be as if a brightly coloured bauble attracts your attention, fascinates you, and you feel that you have to have it; your emotional desires project outwards and you are pulled along with them to the object – only to discover after a temporary possession and perusal that it is not that fascinating after all; yet in that intense drive to achieve your short-lived desire, you may have caused problems and suffering for others. This can apply especially within relationships, where a tendency to desire new partners, experimentation and promiscuity can occur. Your love-life is unlikely to be static and stable. The need to have your own way – often expressed without due sensitivity – is quite common, and also can lead to friction.

Children are likely to play an important role in your life, and you are liable to give them considerable freedom, which can have dual effects, especially if there is a reluctance to impose discipline upon them and you fail to give them sufficient attention and guidance for their needs.

Temperamentally, you are likely to have an artistic ability and appreciation. Natural talents can be present in art, music, literature and for self-presentation through modern media channels of communication. There may be some degree of blockage in this area, which could reflect a lack of perseverance and discipline, rather than problems in confidence in your own ability or potential skills. It is the commitment to complete that can be a challenge for you, as you prefer that sense of freedom to follow your fascinations whenever they dominate you. Uranus intends that a change in this sphere of life is necessary, where modifying this tendency can eventually lead to success.

URANUS IN THE 6TH HOUSE

The basic themes of challenges and opportunities for change in this house are associated with work, service and health.

Due to the Uranian reaction to the imposition of repetitive, mundane tasks, there may be adult difficulties in the sphere of employment, especially in enjoying and maintaining a job. The need for stimulation and real interest in the work is essential, otherwise you are likely to experience considerable dissatisfaction and frustration in your working environment, which can lead to periodic changes of job and employment instability. Even during your childhood, this could manifest as a lack of persistence and prolonged attention to your lessons; even though you may be a bright child, fluctuations of concentration and application are liable to have a detrimental effect on your scholastic progress.

You will need as much freedom as possible in the work sphere, and would certainly resent a high degree of supervision. What you will probably have to learn and develop over time is an ability to be more mentally concentrated on the task before you, and a greater degree of self-discipline in using your mind in productive and practical ways. The tendency can be to live too much in ideas, and fail to actualise them.

There may be the ability to work well with modern technology, through scientific developments or computer-derived employment. There will be an interest in technological advancement, as this appeals to the futurist dimension of Uranus. It is likely that becoming satisfied in this area of life may take some time to achieve, and changes in work or career directions are to be expected.

Your health can be another source of personal change. Your physical body may have periodic illnesses, perhaps caused by the response to the highly stimulatory and agitating Uranus energy. Or possibly some form of a serious or incapacitating illness may suddenly occur, disrupting your lifestyle. This may not be as negative as it appears; there is likely to be the opportunity of a hidden potential path, which if recognised and followed could lead to a positive transformation in your life. This could unfold into personal experience of alternate unconventional health therapies (which today are proliferating and taking firm root within society). You could gain relief from illness through such an approach based on holistic concepts of healing, or you could become interested in training in such skills. This can lead to a totally new way of living and perceiving life, and this could be the intention of the Uranus stimulus.

Such a development could become the way in which your relationship to others deepens, either through sharing these unorthodox healing ideas or through becoming an actual practitioner. If you become a healer, then you may need to regulate your energy flow more, so that the erratic Uranian vibration is not so noticeable, but the electric nature of that energy could be extremely useful especially when involved in techniques such as massage, manipulation or auric healing, which require physical contact. Certainly any knowledge of body regulators and adjusters through herbs, homoeopathy, acupuncture, etc., could help you considerably in modifying inner stress and tension created by the highly strung Uranus vibration. Through aiding others, you could discover a satisfying form of work which fulfils your needs.

URANUS IN THE 7TH HOUSE

Uranus in this natal house will be active in the sphere of personal relationships, where it is most unlikely that you will experience smooth-running, tranquil partnerships.

Often, this becomes a struggle over the issue of relatedness, and what that actually involves and demands from people. Everyone has to undergo some kind of adjustment and modification of their behaviour within all social relationships, perhaps more intensely within intimate partnerships or marriage when people live together. You may find such changes difficult to make, or resent having to do so, and this reflects that Uranian tendency to be highly individual and rebellious. With that stubborn obstinacy and belief in being right, you may fail to even see why you have to adjust in order for a relationship to continue and prosper. Certainly the question of freedom will rise, and your insistence on this and having your own way is likely to create conflict. At times, an insensitivity to the parallel 'rights' of others can stand out in stark relief to some of your progressive social ideas.

Commitment is another problem area. You probably have severe mood changes, attitudes and interests can rise and fall with surprising rapidity; often your demand for freedom and individual expression is but a cover for this inner fluctuation, as you know how erratic and unpredictable you can be. Coupled with this is that urge for new stimulation, perhaps new partners, and the thought of willingly tying yourself to one person can frighten you through fear of restriction and limitation. Running away from relationships of any depth can indeed restrict you to experiencing only superficial affairs.

Many changes in your life will be triggered by the nature and outcome of your social and intimate relationships. There may be sudden affairs, marriages, divorces, due to unpredictable behaviour by either yourself or others. Your life can be turned upside down in such situations, and even your demands for freedom in a relationship could suddenly become freedom without any partner! These relationships will probably have an element of the unorthodox about them, with unconventional and unusual experiences likely, especially if you are inclined to cross the lines of social taboos.

You may need to discover, and clarify for yourself, the function of relationship in society, to look at how you handle your relationships and how you regard their purpose. Uranus is attempting to lead you towards a new understanding of relationship in life, so that you can find real freedom within the relationship web instead of always being tempted to break out and stand alone. You need to transcend that aspect of destructiveness that you often bring into a relationship, which makes you respond to the pressure of growth by deciding that the tensions are unresolvable and looking for ways to shatter the bonds. In fact, a new approach to this sphere of life could open doors to entirely new forms of relationship, where each live together in relative harmony, yet are free enough to follow their own independent paths in a spirit of conscious partnership, instead of any antagonistic self-seeking demands which are exclusive of the partner, and which ignore their needs and sensitivities. If you can successfully modify your natural tendencies, relationships of valuable depth can be possible, which as you mature would really fulfil your needs.

URANUS IN THE 8TH HOUSE

There are several ways in which the influence of the natal Uranus can work through an 8th house position. These can range from a focus on material possessions and money, through to an interest in the worlds hidden behind the material appearance.

This can also involve a crisis of the relationship between self and others; a new understanding and expression is probably required in order for a new light to reveal new potentialities. It is a deeper process of social relating that can be explored, where there is a wider scope for the insights to be displayed and communicated.

Underlying this are the themes of transiency, of death and rebirth. Changes can be triggered in your life which are reflective of these themes. There may be sudden legacies, perhaps due to a family bereavement, which in the pain of loss can also offer opportunities to another. Business ventures or marriages may collapse, reminding you that nothing in life is for ever. The realisation of change, that life and loved ones can slip through one's grasp like grains of sand, can radically disturb any sense of inner security, especially one which is founded on material principles.

It is certain that you will lose something or someone of importance in your life, and that will be the catalyst for the process of searching to begin. It is a questioning to discover if there is any solid foundation in life, or how to deal

with this transiency which when experienced in a negative form can strip the life of all colour and vitality. What is needed then is a rebirth, through which, with wiser attitudes, you are more ready to face the facts of life. This rebirth can occur through an investigation into the hidden inner realities beyond the superficial appearances. This can be through scientific or occult investigations, where the sense of probing new dimensions can stimulate and excite the mind. Yet it is often a maturation of your emotional level that is required, so that you are able to commence deeper relationships with others too. This rebirth is not just a personal need, it is tied in with the nature of your social relationships, where personal development should also have beneficial social repercussions. In finding a new self, you should also realise a new form of social relating, expressing your place and function within the webbing of the collective network.

Sexuality can also be an aspect of your nature that Uranus seeks to work changes through. The importance of sexual activity may be quite strong in your life, possibly determining certain choices for you as a result of its demanding voice. Uranus will stimulate an unconventional approach to this fact of adult life, and your scope in this sphere could be considerable and varied. This will be especially so if aspects are made to natal Moon, Venus and Mars. Your sexuality can add to the forming and dissolution of partnerships, and depending on their impact in your life, Uranus may take this route to confront you with its necessary lessons. This could even include moving beyond a certain emotional detachment and distancing, towards more embracing, intense, emotional experiences in relationships. Achieving this could result in a rebirth for you in an important sphere of your life.

URANUS IN THE 9TH HOUSE

What Uranus is attempting to guide you towards in this 9th house position, is a revolutionary change in your world-views. Similar to everyone else in your culture and society, you will have grown up under the influence of collective thought-forms, attitudes and beliefs. These will have formed the conditioning social concepts arising from religious, philosophical/moral and educative teachings which form the structure of your society. This is the process of socialising, where the young child is taught how to live within the socially accepted parameters of that culture. Most individuals' thinking is basically repeating what they have been conditioned to think; very few become 'free minds'. Yet such an approach does instil order into society, historical traditions and established patterns of thought being inherited and transmitted across generations.

But it is in the fixity of such mental patterns that problems arise. They inhibit explorative discovery, leading to branding such thinkers as heretical; they suppress questioning of the status quo, creating dissidents, who are leant on by the weight of the State; they deny and inhibit necessary changes from occurring, in case the results are destabilising; they ignore the consequences of choices made under these fixed world/cultural views, because if they do not, the edifices of their political/religious beliefs collapse through being revealed as outdated and inappropriate.

What Uranus will expect is that you break out of these restricting mental paradigms. There is probably a spirit of revolution in you anyway, inclining you to free expression of your own unique individuality; but Uranus in the 9th house will fuel this need, so that you can mentally breathe freely instead of suffocating. This certainly will not be an easy move to make, as it involves shaking off the accumulated dust of centuries of that society's thinking, in order to gain a glimpse of something else that has perhaps been lost. The problem is that until an individual wakes to the fact of this social conditioning, it is not realised how deep its effects have grown. Most of the sense of personal identity is rooted in that ground, the reflective angles of self-perception have been allowed only within a certain social context, and the rest are 'taboo areas' where social constraint is attempted over even words and thoughts.

If you can achieve a new mental paradigm, a way of experiencing and perceiving the nature of life, then you will have been truly reborn. Through you could come advanced, progressive, utopian ideas and visions (reflecting the Ideation of Uranus); you could become inspirational to others who are seeking ways out of the impasse facing them. Expressions such as teaching and publishing could become your 'outbreath' released into the world to continue and stimulate the process of change and liberation. But it will not be easy to have the roots of your mind and identity uprooted, and then replanted to give a totally new scenario of the universe. One can start by pausing, looking within and considering what you do really think and know. Has it been absorbed through forms of conditioning? Essentially ask yourself the question 'Who am I, and what am I doing here?'. The 'answer' can be an ongoing experience, the start of your personal revolution.

URANUS IN THE 10TH HOUSE

The challenges confronting you with this placement are involved with your relationship to society, and your role and function within the collective expression of your generation. This will concern personal desires and the expression of your individual tendencies, as well as a potential social contribution that you may make.

There is likely to be an inner impulse to succeed and to rise socially, gaining prestige, status, authority, power and influence. Applying your strong will may make this quite possible, but much will depend upon the sometimes unpredictable Uranian activity, and whether this will undermine your conscious efforts. You may be quite able to organise yourself well, and progress through discipline and work, but much will depend on your sense of social relationship and obligation.

If the thrust of your desire is purely personal, for ego gratification, power over others, social status, or monetary gain, and fails to take due regard for others or the social consequences of your decisions, then Uranus may conspire to prevent further progress, perhaps through the influence of others in your social circles or by allowing you to over-emphasise several of your more damaging characteristics through hubris. This can often occur in business or political scenes, where the dynamics of the élite power structures can be difficult to handle successfully. Your ambition could be thwarted, perhaps through a Uranian lack of deference for an employer or authority senior to you in the hierarchy.

Often, your relation to authority can be difficult and touchy, and your feelings towards power can be ambiguous. An adjustment may be required in these feelings, so that you are able to develop your own personal power, instead of probably inhibiting it to some degree. If you can accept your own power, then your attitudes and understanding of the roles and functions of authorities and power will also change.

You will be really looking to discover your own role and function in society, a process of potential integration into the whole. You could fail, and become a reactionary revolutionary, feeding off rejected negative energies, and primarily being destructive rather than constructive in your response to your own failure.

Yet the most appropriate way could be the pioneering of new ways and concepts, where liberal humanitarian and radical social politics attract you, satisfying the Uranian impulse for future-orientated social change. As usual, you will demand as much freedom as possible in your life, stalking around like a caged animal if it is denied. This need could develop into an unusual career or profession, which can absorb such a demand without any detriment, and it may be that over time your innovative perspective could lead you to become a leader or spokesperson for some idealistic cause or scientific development. This will depend on that ability to generate personal power and to apply it in a socially influential manner, and this is unlikely to happen overnight but emerge as a consequence of effort and persistence in a chosen direction.

URANUS IN THE 11TH HOUSE

Whilst the 5th house is concerned with personal creativity, the 11th house is concerned with the social dimension of group consciousness and creativity, and with changes in the dominating social paradigm of your civilisation and culture. Uranus will be guiding you towards involvement in group co-operation which is designed to achieve common social ideals or philosophies, which it is believed could help society to function better and encourage people to have more satisfying lives. Obviously this can create a situation of conflict with other groupings who have different views.

You are likely to feel part of a social movement, one which is probably humanitarian, libertarian and attuned to the ideals of world brother and sisterhood, the 'One Family of Mankind'. If Uranus can be fluently expressed through this placing (i.e. harmonious aspects), then you may be open-minded and receptive to the Higher Collective/Universal Mind, intuitively grasping the outpouring of the overshadowing source of progressive seed ideas. In alliance with others, you can determine your social role, which is probably to give a collective voice to reformist ideas, as the whole 'speaks' through a unified group consciousness, and reveals its underlying purpose and evolutionary intention to humanity.

Such group involvement, on the inner or outer planes, will be a central factor in your life, offering direction, discipline and meaning. Many of your social friendships will emerge from these group associations. Yet problems can occur if Uranus has challenging aspects, and these can emerge through such relationships or a desire to be highly individualistic to the detriment of a group purpose. The urge for freedom and a questionable degree of commitment can stimulate such problems, which will also reoccur in your more intimate relationships. Sometimes, that degree of impersonality can spoil potentially successful relationships when, in responding to that siren call of 'freedom', your commitment collapses and your interest wanes in favour of exploring the new horizons. Also, you may need to guard against supporting irresponsible and impractical beliefs and ideas, which can appeal to that aspect of mental eccentricity that often goes hand in hand with the high Uranian ideologies.

URANUS IN THE 12TH HOUSE

Uranus in this house involves the concepts of endings, transitions, the results of the past, and an affinity with the unconscious mind. In several ways, this can be a challenging placement, which will oblige you to confront powerful hidden habit patterns or 'karmic residues' which are affecting your life, options and choices.

There is a parallel between your psychological health and that of society, through the connections of the collective and individual unconscious mind. Often you will be pulled back towards the past, both because of the influence that it has on your current life, and as an escape from the present moment. Emotionally, you probably have 'unfinished business' with the past, and perhaps with parental relationships. There will be a need to free yourself from this preoccupation, and to resolve the stresses and splits that make you look back; such an integration could become essential for your psychological well-being, and if problems develop related to your mental interpretation of human 'reality', you may need psychotherapy (even self-directed) to enable you to release the unconscious pressures, and to shine a liberating light clarifying and making the unconscious conscious. Forms of self-evasion and deception may work at covering up inner splits and problems for a time, but eventually they will stand revealed, as the personality-structure fragments under the strain of living an illusion.

In discovering self-healing, one participates and contributes to the healing of the collective. The higher aspect of this placement includes the potential to become an inspirational channel and voice of the collective mind, the natural inner receptivity being expressed in forms of insight, revelation and artistic creativity. This may emerge after a period of self-exploration, through which a more inclusive centre of identity and consciousness is discovered as previously unconscious aspects of the self are exposed to the light.

You will certainly have to face the consequences of the dominating patterns which are operating through your life. Wherever these derive from, or from whichever experiences they have been formed, you will initially have to acknowledge their existence and impact on you; accepting them as part of you is the next step in integration, and will begin to resolve their more negative influences. A serious evaluation of these restrictions and limitations may reveal their potential transcending too, indicating the right way forward. Confronting 'fate' is not inevitably a negative encounter; it can equally be the opening of the doors of opportunity and success, and a sowing of fruitful seeds for the commencement of the next cycle of experience and expression.

CHAPTER 6

Transit Cycles of Uranus

THE TOTAL TRANSIT CYCLE of Uranus lasts for a time-span of approximately eighty-four years. Several additional cyclic patterns stem from this concerning the aspects made by the planet and its movement through the signs and houses. The actual time of the transit cycle is closer to 83 years, 9 months and 3 days. Despite the astrological façade of calculative precision, it is more rewarding to consider the cycle to be a round eighty-four years. As any astrologer should recognise through comparisons between ephemerides and computer-calculated planetary positions, common agreement can often be lacking on certain positions, especially with the faster-moving planets and the Ascendant degree.

During the full transit cycle, Uranus will conjunct and oppose each planet once, and will make the square, sextile and trine aspects twice. Uranus will move direct for approximately seven months, then retrograde for the following five months, over a yearly cycle. At the change of station, if Uranus makes an aspect to a natal planet, then this is likely to be repeated three times. Uranus will transit through each sign every seven years.

There are three major cycles associated with the whole Uranus transit. These are the seven-year cycle, the twenty-eight-year cycle, and the twelve cycles each of seven years each through the signs and houses.

THE SEVEN–YEAR CYCLE

This can be a simple yet revealing short cycle to use in interpretations, offering a pattern of development that can easily be successfully applied to adult living and phases of personal expression. There can be repetitive patterns occurring in a life which correspond to this cycle, and these can reflect an ongoing confrontation with personality aspects that still require resolving by a greater self-understanding. These may also coincide with aspects made by the transiting Uranus with natal planets, especially those which are of a more challenging nature, like the square and opposition and some non-complementary conjunctions. For instance, a first marriage made at the age of 21 at the time of the first year of the cycle, falls apart and the couple separate by the age of 27. One of the partners enters into a new stable relationship at 28, and then by 35 that second marriage begins to enter a new phase. This displays a repetitive theme, although the nature of the process changes through greater awareness and wiser choices, through to the point at 35 where the relationship enters a rebirth phase, instead of collapsing as previously.

Within this seven-year cycle, each year acts as a symbol for a distinct phase of the full cycle for the personal life. It indicates what will be the general emerging trends and level of individual meaning and activity which can lead to the maximum degree of success, if right harmony is made with the cycle. Each 'year' commences at the birthday, and is concluded by the following birthday. An interesting exercise can be made in comparing a personal life pattern to this unfolding pattern. A personal review can reveal an affinity to this cycle whereby the events and life experiences correspond very closely; if this is so, then it is wise to consider future life in the light of this guide. The first year begins at birth. The ages at which subsequent years begin are indicated below.

Year of cycle Age at which year begins

1st	7, 14, 21, 28, 35, 42, 49, 56, 63, 70 , 77, 84
2nd	1, 8, 15, 22, 29, 36, 43, 50, 57, 64, 71, 78
3rd	2, 9, 16, 23, 30, 37, 44, 51, 58, 65, 72, 79
4th	3, 10, 17, 24, 31, 38, 45, 52, 59, 66, 73, 80
5th	4, 11, 18, 25, 32, 39, 46, 53, 60, 67, 74, 81
6th	5, 12, 19, 26, 33, 40, 47, 54, 61, 68, 75, 82
7th	6, 13, 20, 27, 34, 41, 48, 55, 62, 69, 76, 83

1st Year

The 1st year is the release of the new conditioning impulse, which will set the tone for the rest of the cycle. This impulse will be definitely connected to the seeding at the end of the previous cycle during the 7th year. You are likely to be unsure about the nature of this new impulse, as there will be a lack of conscious clarity and an evasiveness about firmly grasping the new direction until you can be sure of its reality. You will sense that something new and unexplored is stirring within you, and this can stimulate both feelings of fear and unease and hopes for broader opportunities to exploit.

Psychologically, you will be 'Janus-faced', looking back into the recent past and forward into the future simultaneously. In fact, there is probably some event or experience that occurred during the 7th year or early in this new phase that contained the seed-essence of this new direction. However, at this point, you will feel the imminent need for change, but be unsure and confused over how to satisfy this, and which direction to take. It is a problem of options and choices, and in many cases, there will be a reluctance to make an early decision.

Emotionally, you may feel vulnerable and a little unstable, which is caused by this inner agitation, and emotional flux and volatility is likely. Until you begin to feel more secure and confident in the direction in which you wish to travel, you will be reticent. In a minority of cases, there can be a great feeling of freedom, a releasing of limitation which offers the enjoyment of actualising latent potential through confident experimentation and opening new doors. It can be viewed as a year of preparation and inner rebalancing.

2nd Year

This is a year of choice, whether to respond actively to the changes embodied within the new impulse, or to react against its impact upon your life. Positive response can lead to discovering a renewed vitality and direction in life, which could affect all levels of your nature and your lifestyle; or you can be resistant to change through fear and unwillingness to restructure yourself and your lifestyle. Such an inner inertia can oppose the new impulse, creating a state of friction, conflict, and stress. You will need to find some way to minimise inner discomfort and tension, and the power of the new impulse will slowly seek to erode these foundations of resistance.

Challenges may arise in areas of your social and financial life, or personal psychological difficulties can occur, and as these are likely to require clear decisions, your solutions also have to be committed as they will affect your choices in the remainder of this cycle. It is probably wiser to bow to the inevitability of change, rather than to waste energy and time in futile reaction.

3rd Year

By now, the nature of the impulse for this cycle should be clear and defined; the direction should be recognised, and you are likely to have made several inner/outer adaptations necessary to be capable of responding to its promptings. Co-operation with the impulse should involve definite actions taken in order to manifest its transformative quality in the destined sphere of its activities. Whilst you may feel that you are incapable of fully achieving this impulse, perhaps through a lack of personal ability, confidence or means, you should ensure that you try to do so to the greatest extent possible. Efforts made now could bear fruit at the parallel stage of the next cycle, or even result in a more immediate success than you believed possible or were expecting.

4th Year

There is a turning-point around 3 years 6 months, when the impulse has reached a point of materialising and actualising through the individual. The growth below the ground in the dark has been completed, and now the impulse can emerge into the light of day. New opportunities and challenges will occur, and it is a year of crisis in that through application and hard work, the impulse can be fully embodied and then is resistant to the pull of inertia that has so far restricted its emergence. Ideally, the 'new' will have defeated the old outworn patterns. Hidden within this year, there will be a crucial point of choice, which may be obvious or veiled as to its real implications. It will involve a decision that cannot be avoided, but which is connected to the essence of the emerging impulse. This decisive choice will have powerful repercussions on your life and future options.

5th Year

Potentially, this could be the year when – as a result of your successful prior efforts in this cycle – you make a breakthrough in your attempts at self-expression and following your own direction. The theme, message and purpose of the impulse should be realised with clarity and intensity. This will be founded upon the work and visualisation of the 3rd year, and can enable you to develop more rapidly and consciously, and the seed will be transformed into a 'flower'. There will be a social dimension to this, and you may begin to share with others more, acting as a point of radiating influence and a guide or leader in some respect. However, if you have adopted a more resistant position, this year could see the dissolution of many of your dreams and hopes, as the energy is unable to revitalise them.

6th Year

This can be a year of achievement and fulfilment, which can also contain a need to relinquish or sacrifice something as a form of propitiation for the gifts of the gods. At the time of success, there can also be loss, and a reminder of the impermanence of life, which can encourage you to gain a wider perspective, and to inwardly dedicate your talents to the successful fulfilment of future cycles.

You may sense an undercurrent of deep agitation, perhaps a feeling of frustration or dissatisfaction hidden within the results of success, possibly the loss of something important to you. There is an ambiguity; within success lies the seed of failure, and within failure lies the seed of success, reflecting the polarisation of human life, and the belief that within every action lies an equal and opposite reaction.

7th Year

This is the year of conclusion, and the formation of the new seeds for the next cycle. A sense of new change will be registered, a need for new or modified values and directions to pursue. The results of the seven-year cycle will now be recognised; relative success or relative failure. New opportunities will be present to expand into new horizons. If you moved with the changes before, then you should accept the next impulse and co-operate with that too, because now you know that in doing so, some success is made at least. If you resisted it the last time, then here is a new opportunity to make some progress in re-orientating your inner and outer life. From this year, the new seed will be formed, and it is wiser to take this chance to sow as positive and bright a future cycle for yourself as possible.

Twelve Cycles of Seven Years

The Uranus transit moves through each sign every seven years. Each of these sign transits could be sub-divided into seven yearly phases as represented by the previous seven-year cyclic pattern. If this is done, then the associative changes of Uranus transiting through the signs offers a working approach to gain the maximum personal benefit of the intended transformation.

The Aries year corresponds to the period from birth till the age of 7, and the 1st house of identity. This involves physical birth, the awakening of innate instinctual and personality patterns, and the gradual process of differentiation and separation from the parents into a distinct identity.

The Taurus year corresponds to the period from age 7 to 14 and the 2nd house of resources. This involves the awakening of the separative self into matter, and the dawning of emotional and sexual feelings and puberty. The latter part of this 'year' commences the confusing time of hormonal adolescent changes, and overlaps with the next cycle.

The Gemini year corresponds to ages 14 to 21, and the 3rd house of communication. This is the process of socialisation and the conscious learning of suitable life skills prior to entering the adult life. There is more of a mental awakening at this time, and a social demand to be more 'grown up', rational and capable of using the mind effectively, both in being able to contribute to society through work and in communication with others.

The Cancer year corresponds to ages 21 to 28 and the 4th house of foundations. Here the young adult is expected to put down 'roots', possibly marry and establish their own separate home and family. It is an acceptance of the demands made by contemporary society, and involves conformism and a probable limiting of freedom and options.

The Leo year corresponds to ages 28 to 35, and the 5th house of children, self-expression and creativity. This implies a new phase of greater potential freedom, where the parental influence has now waned, and the likely birth of one's own children has evoked a more adult way of life. Social adaptation should be sufficient now to allow for a more self-decisive movement towards greater personal choices of creativity and unique individuality. This point can reflect the start of a life turning-point; the individual begins to look seriously for a lifestyle which he wants, rather than one which has been unconsciously socially programmed into him.

The Virgo year corresponds to ages 35 to 42, and the 6th house of work, health and service. This is the halfway point, and continues that potential re-orientation with a new evaluation of the personal lifestyle, attitudes, and work patterns, to determine if these still fit and satisfy. At this phase, between the ages of 38–42, the transiting Uranus will make an opposition to its natal position, and so stimulate the traditional 'mid-life crisis', which can erupt into any expression of life where the need for change is the greatest, or where the personal stability and confidence is at its weakest.

The Libra year corresponds to ages 42 to 49, and the 7th house of relationships. This can fall into the opposition aspect, and is a turning-point of the cycle, and one where the inner balance is likely to swing violently at times from a point of equilibrium. The Uranus energy makes it even harder to discover that point of balance, and often dissatisfaction within relationships and long-standing marriages occurs, adding a destabilising factor. It is necessary to discover new ways of relating, both within the personal inner life and with those closest intimates, in order to revitalise possibly stagnating relationships.

2/96

The Scorpio year corresponds to ages 49 to 56, and the 8th house of regeneration and rebirth. Here one is faced with signs of impending mortality, perhaps as parents die, grandchildren are born, and the body begins to show signs of use. Choices become more limited, as radical life changes are harder to make, partly through deeply grooved established habit patterns and economic constraints. Youth is lost, and self-confidence in sexual attractiveness can dissolve, leaving a void in personal perception, confusion in relationships, and emotional conflicts over a variety of inner changes occurring. An acceptance of the ageing process is needed. A rebirth into the next phase needs to be achieved.

The Sagittarius year corresponds to ages 56 to 63, and the 9th house. During this time, transiting Uranus makes a square to its natal position between the ages of 58 to 62, and inner adaptations are required to ease the build-up of tension. It can be a time of harvesting the results of a lifetime of effort in self-unfoldment, and potentially a new birth into the latter phases of the cycle and life. This can be a release from the confines of work, allowing time to enjoy personal interests more, self-reflection and freedom from a now grown-up family. Around the age of 56, the trine made by transiting Uranus to its natal position can stimulate an inner rebirth directed towards more spiritual concerns, or where the struggle to accept the inevitability of death has to be inwardly resolved.

The following three years of Capricorn, Aquarius and Pisces correspond to ages 63 to 70, 70 to 77 and 77 to 84, and houses 10 to 12 respectively. These are the peak and culmination of the life, prior to any new, more transcendent cycle commencing after the age of 84. Here, most of the seed patterns of the life should have been expressed, explored and exploited. The quality of the real inner life should be at its most potent, concentrated and powerful, with the richness and wisdom accrued from experience. The real unique individuality can be revealed more clearly as the veils of matter become more translucent and penetrable to the light of the indwelling spirit, especially if the individual has followed a spiritual, transpersonal life. It is a phase of resolving unfinished business, of life endings and abstracting the vital energies.

The twenty-eight-year cycle is related to the transits of Uranus, and to the potentiality for three 'births' to occur in a life dedicated to spiritual unfoldment. The first birth is that of the physical body, the point of incarnation into life on earth, the materialisation of the 'idea'. The second can occur around the age of 28, when transiting Uranus makes a trine aspect to its natal position, which also corresponds to the Leo year and the potential for releasing the true unique individuality. For some, this can correspond with a spiritual rebirth, which sets the direction for the remainder of the life. The third, around the age of 56, has been previously mentioned, and is more likely to occur if the previous step was made at 28. In essence, these reflect the birth and development of self (0 to 28 years); the demand to externalise and be that whole self (28 to 56); and the resulting integration and transcendence of self (56 to 84). These phases do not have to correspond with the pattern of ages, yet can often be very accurate.

Uranus fulfils his role as the Awakener, and this function is dynamically expressed through his impact on the individual as the transit cycle progresses. Every one will have their life affected by Uranus as it moves through the houses and aspects natal planets, and it is of value to understand the nature and quality of this powerful energy, become aware of its style of activity within the individual and to discover how best to respond positively.

For those who are especially inwardly sensitive, the movement of Uranus can be intuited when it is within 2 or 3 degrees of an exact aspect with a natal planet, which could be two or three months previously. Unless that individual is an astrologer who has calculated the planetary positions, and is monitoring his own unfolding pattern and so anticipating the recognised Uranus transit, this will be felt as an inner disquiet, a tension or pressure build-up reflected in a need to change. It is a sense of 'something going on' beyond the volition or conscious control of that individual, and a stirring in the unconscious mind. This can have an ominous quality, a fear of losing control where there is the deep shaking of existing personality foundations. Possibly there may be a distinct awareness of the appropriate sphere of life that is destined to be transformed (through Uranian transit into that house), and a recognition of necessary change.

The eventual point of crisis can happen at the time of the exact aspect being made, and this can be quite powerful and traumatic, especially if it involves the sudden breaking down of an established way of life or relationship. Yet this point will have been building up for some time. It can be useful to consider transiting charts from a Uranus standpoint, and to note the times of entering a 3 degrees from aspect phase. If this is imminent in a client's chart, then it can be indicated to them, and expressed in terms of likely areas of impact. For instance, a transiting Uranus aspect to natal Venus will influence the nature of any close or intimate relationships and can lead to changes in personal feelings, demands for greater freedom, more sexual variety, or a sense of being trapped in an unsatisfying marriage. A transformation of some kind is required in that area of life.

Uranus acts to renew life, whether this is consciously desired or not, and will break those repetitive patterns of lifestyle and personality that are effectively inhibiting a fuller experience of the scope of life. Its style of revolution serves to add an element of chaos and disorganisation which dissolves the cohesiveness of established patterns prior to a reassembly which allows a new phase of growth. Potential is stimulated, whilst simultaneously offering clarity into the current stagnation of the present life situation in the associated sphere. Once that inner lightning bolt has illuminated the mind and emotions, any repressed area of dissatisfaction becomes unavoidably conscious, thus emphasising the need for change. The sense of frustration and lack of meaning sits there as if in an uncomfortable position, refusing to be ignored.

Uranus gives new life to all those hidden thoughts, desires and feelings that have been pushed down into the dark during the past. These can be desires for certain types of experiences that have not been lived out, or they can coincide with ideas and intentions that have been previously thought about but not actualised. Nothing that Uranus will bring through into conscious confrontation is 'new' to the individual; its genesis will have been formulated prior to its emergence as an active demand. What can also emerge are patterns of resistance, denials of the process of change, denials of self. These clash with the impulse to live and act out personal needs, as they have to become real. Whichever choice of action the individual makes, the results are inevitable; something is irrevocably changed in the process.

The stimulation of Uranus is like an electrical charge, speedy, restless, an intensification in the experiencing and perception of daily living, a feeling of inexorable movement propelling the person towards a dark unknown. It is a need for freedom from a suffocating lifestyle, a need to find the exit in order to breathe freely again. It may be an urge to destroy in order to be renewed. For some, it can feel like a wild animal, caged and pacing around in its prison, growing more bad-tempered as it fails to find freedom, its energy hitting the walls of its enclosure and bouncing back to be turned upon itself. People can have more freedom than such an animal, yet often fail to change willingly without an outer pressure forcing them.

Uranus becomes our 'fate' when personal efforts to change are either not made or are insufficient to be effective. From the outer world, circumstances conspire to create those situations which we have to confront and experience. A marriage partner suddenly announces that they are leaving, a notice of redundancy is received, our political or religious beliefs and ideals are shocked by new insights or revelations about our favourite political leader or religious guru, a business collapses with outstanding debts, family deaths... We attract whatever is necessary for us to conform with the inner pattern which is unfolding through our lives. Some may call it 'karma', the reaping of past seeds of 'good and evil' actions.

Whatever we have outgrown, as comfortable as it may be, is liable to be a target for Uranus. He ends life phases, and initiates the next one. The conjunction aspect made by transiting Uranus to a natal planet offers a powerful release of inner energy, which often seems to parallel a culmination or climax of a phase, and the birth of a new cycle. Crossing the angles also acts in a similar way, although what is normally more evident within the consciousness is the 'death process' of endings rather than the new beginnings. In the chaos of the transition phase, the individual can be cast adrift on a sea of their own freed impulses, being erratic, uncontrolled, selfish and individual only in the sense of spontaneously responding to the dominant urges of the moment. This inner 'possession' of liberated energy leads to eventual statements of 'I didn't know what I was doing, but I had to do it . . .', 'I just had to walk out . . . I didn't really think about it . . .'. Such points are characterised by personal instability, lack of awareness for others, and an overriding urge to reassert independence and individuality – the expression of which often seems quite out of character.

The urge to destroy can be hard to moderate. Most people would have little idea of what is happening to them, let alone act to redirect this impulse into potentially positive channels designed to transform the life in a self-creative way. Many break away from existing lives just to enter a period of being 'lost', the mooring ropes thrown away and no land in sight, sailing freely with the wind, but lacking any real direction to travel in, or reason for doing so. Some project their inner anger and frustration at close partners, subjecting them to a collapsing relationship and blaming them for everything that offers discontent. Sometimes a form of apathy results through denial, and the life structures fall because no one is maintaining them.

Letting go and trusting in the process is often hard for people. It requires a faith in life which many find difficult to believe. What is happening is a natural form of growth, which is always unsettling and confusing, especially to a personality that is focused in a concept of egoistic continuity and has built a fixed lifestyle to amplify that fragile feeling. A social educational development towards the reality of a 'multiplicity of selves' and to a mutable ever-changing concept of individuality and personality could help to alleviate such problems.

Eventually, these growing pains will diminish as the first shoots of the replacement seeds of the new direction emerge above the surface of consciousness. These are seeds of hope and potential, and involve the activity of creating the future by actions and choices taken in the present. These 'seeds' could be received as internal guidance or messages, an intuition of the direction to take, or as an outpouring of new ideas which can be applied to transform life. The process of cultivating all these seeds may span several years, or even the remainder of the lifetime, and there can be a sense of impatience at the implied time-span and the slowness of change.

Often the opposition aspects made by the transiting Uranus with a natal planet can correspond with points of major decisions which are dependent upon the quality of awareness in determining the choices taken. An opposition made with the natal Sun can trigger an enquiry into the nature of the personal identity and purpose, which can result in radical inner changes being made which eventually create a new lifestyle and relationship with life.

Often, the individual undergoing the disruption of an activating Uranus will just want to run away from all of the problems and challenges that seem to confront him. There doesn't seem to be an adequate inner strength to cope successfully. But instead of attempting to disassociate with the past and the present, a wiser approach that can be made by a person familiar with the process is to work to bring appropriate changes within the existing life structure. This can add some stability and continuity, and offer a channel for the energies to move into; there is no divine fiat that dictates that the whole life has to be shattered into fragments. That will only happen as a result of opposition, and as the last resort of a blocked Uranus energy.

The challenges which face the individual parallel similar ones within the wider society. Most people resist change, and they often also fail to have any understanding of what is happening within them. Their personal ignorance and unconsciousness of the inner life is often quite deep, and they often mask the choppy inner waters by pretending that 'everything is all right really'. Otherwise, if they accept that a problem exists, they tell themselves that it will just go away if they avoid thinking about it. Pressure mounts as the dam walls begin to strain, and the unconscious mind attracts outer experiences and situations that synchronise with the purpose of its inner activity. Tensions build until there is the recognition that something has to be done to change an untenable position. Usually the greatest 'shocks' to the edifice occur during the early penetration into a new house placement, setting the tone or message that Uranus is bearing.

Individually, the inner questions accumulate. How can I become free? What do I need to change in myself or my life in order to be liberated? What direction do I want to travel in, and how can I do this whilst still fulfilling present obligations and family commitments? How can I successfully move from this current lifestyle into one that would really suit me? And would I be supported by my family? What risks am I able to take, so that the 'dream' can be realised? Am I capable of success? It is like a crucifixion between the choices of the past which are embodied in the present, and the magnetic attraction of the unknown future which appears to promise 'heart's desires'. And during this time, catalysts appear to move you in certain directions. They can appear as old ideas suddenly reborn with fresh vitality, old dreams that could be experienced, old friends reappearing to offer potential opportunities, or new acquaintances with new alternative ways of living and perceiving life. If you can recognise the signs, you realise that you are never left alone.

As Uranus transits through the houses, periodic revolutionary change will spread through those spheres of life. Over each seven-year phase, your attitudes and level of understanding will be transmuted, and this will commence early in each transit when that sense of discontent is initially registered, and the corresponding impulse for new horizons rises within consciousness. It is in the houses where cyclically the need of transformation is most urgent, and where effectively you will rebel against your self-imposed restrictions. In your own nature, you will repeat the twofold struggle of Uranus–Saturn, whereby Saturn first overthrows Uranus to impose materialistic order, and Uranus attempts to subvert Saturn's boundaries in order to liberate new life.

It will probably take a period of between two and two and a half years to begin integrating the meaning and relevance of a Uranian transit aspect, especially as certain aspects can be made three times during such a phase, as with conjunctions and direct and retrograde movement over that time. With the transit through the signs and houses, there is a seven-year pattern operating. Sometimes, there seems to be no rest at all from the process of self-development . . . and no escape either!

URANUS TRANSITING 1ST HOUSE

This is the start of a new cycle of transiting Uranus, a cycle which will last for approximately the next eighty-four years. Any new cycle offers the opportunity for a form of rebirth or renewal which is associated with that particular transpersonal planet, and should always be viewed by the individual in terms of potential opportunity, so that the maximum personal benefits can be grasped at the time of offering.

The changes in your life that are likely to emerge during this transit are those which will lay the foundation for the remainder of the full cycle. What will be required of you is real growth towards a fuller expression of the totality of your own unique nature, through which you become more able to visualise and define the scope and content of your imagined and hoped-for future life. Obviously, such a task will demand that you make certain changes in your personal attitudes and values, and at least you will have to confront yourself in the process of determining what your desires, needs, goals and ambitions actually are.

It is likely that the impetus for this approach to self-renewal and enquiry will arise as a result of an inner disturbance, an agitated state of restlessness where you feel that life has lost or is losing its sense of meaning and purpose for you, and that the colour and vitality of existence is fading away. This flatness and lack of stimulation can be the trigger to search for change. It is also quite possible that this trigger can be forced upon you by external circumstances that are beyond your immediate control, such as broader social issues directly impinging on your life, employment difficulties, marital and relationship upheavals, family deaths. Whatever initiates the change, you will have to deal with it inwardly, and this will be the sphere of conflict between the strong existing patterns of habit, behaviour and lifestyle and those inevitable changes that Uranus is seeking to usher into your future life.

To some degree, you will become a disruptive influence as a result of your inner agitation, and this can obviously affect your closer personal relationships especially. This extrusion of your inner conflicts and struggles can intensify the tensions and upset the balance in a relationship, and until you reach an inner point of resolution and clarity, there is relatively little you can do to prevent this 'psychological seepage' influencing those around you. One approach that could help is that of close sharing, whereby you openly acknowledge this inner state of confusion and the impulse to change and find freedom and newness, and choose to co-operate with partners by revealing to them these inner urges and by sharing and living through this process together in mutual understanding and exploration. Otherwise, reacting to the pressures that can build up, you could just strike out into independent action which may release your own tensions but which could create additional strains in the relationship. Or alternatively, your own behaviour and 'changed state' could lead to a breakdown in the relationship initiated by your partner, who may be inwardly objecting to your self-preoccupation, your edgy temperament or lack of interest.

The way that you are likely to benefit most is by consciously searching for new ideas, potentials, experiences and life-directions. This will be disruptive, and as most relationships are based upon repetitive behaviour patterns, can become a negative influence unless an attempt is made to include a partner, otherwise the personal contact will begin to drift apart. You will find that the Uranian energies which are stimulating this trend will offer an in-built positive influence, as in a sense any initial destructive effect will become transformed and nullified as they become fulfilled by creating individual changes and thus fulfilling their function. Take advantage of them, and take any action which your intuition suggests will play a part in your progress towards your envisaged objectives.

If you succeed in clearly defining a future purpose for yourself, then it is more than likely that certain doors will manifest for you to open and pass through. One point to consider is that you do not allow the power of the Uranian influence to make you excessively fanatical or eccentric about your developing personal interests, obsessions or ambitions.

Generally, you will be attracted towards exploring beyond inner barriers; these may be uniquely personal to you, self-imposed or socially conditioned, and can include the urge to go beyond established social attitudes, experiences and traditions. This can lead you towards those dimensions of life which require the development of the intuitive faculty, the 'knowing of things without rational/logical proof or thought'. Meditation or forms of psychological techniques can be useful to develop this ability, and if this can be achieved during this seven-year phase, then the rest of the cycle may take on a totally different outlook for you, being essentially an exploration of a new dimension which can guide your life from within. This connects to the need that you have to express your own uniqueness from an independent position, following your own path wherever it may lead; but you may need to remember that it is necessary to live in good relations with others too, and never to become excessively self-centred in your behaviour, as the appropriate balance has to be found.

URANUS TRANSITING 2ND HOUSE

It is hoped that by now you will have passed through the fundamental changes required for this new cycle, and that the seeds of the future are planted in the ground and that you have a clearer vision of your chosen direction. The 1st house transit can be seen as a preparing of the ground and the first planting of the future seeds.

The process is certainly not completed though, and you may experience an early stage of confusion and bewilderment as this 2nd house transit opens, which still causes you to re-evaluate your direction and attitudes, perhaps to remind you that you are experiencing an ongoing process of perpetual transformation.

The main area of importance at this phase is the sphere of 'personal inheritance', which involves your innate natural talents, abilities and gifts. In some cases, you may find that the Uranian influence acts as a stimulus for previously hidden or unknown talents to display themselves, or a new vitality begins to course through those existing abilities encouraging you to apply your talents more fully or perhaps for the first time.

The direction that you should aim towards is in using these vitalised talents to manifest your chosen purposes, which should have been developed during the 1st house transit. Otherwise, you may lack a clear sense of direction into which you can channel this energy.

It is a time when all your 'inherited possessions' should be applied to produce more practical results, especially those rooted in a more mundane material context. You will need to focus your attention on those areas of life which seem to offer the greatest opportunity for you to express your physical, mental or psychological skills. This may lead you to change certain older, established aspects of your life which seem inappropriate now, especially in the light of your new intentions and ideas of using your talents in a more creative, productive and satisfying manner. This could involve using your savings to start up a new business or to pay for further education and study in order for you to develop additional knowledge, thus creating a foundation for opportunities to open for you later.

Ideally, you should use your abilities so that they can be applied to enhance your quality of life; this could be purely materially, or it could be within a totally personal context, to improve your experience of life by greater self understanding and maturity.

It is a grounding phase of the process, and if you allow yourself to be too erratic or eccentric, then you will find that your energy will drain away instead of being consciously applied to your exploitation of your 'inheritance.'. Personal inertia may pose some problems, but unless you transcend this through self determination, your objectives will remain lifeless and moribund. These tendencies are inevitable, but are not unpassable obstacles.

Initially, it is a phase of 'taking stock' of your 'inheritance and possessions', seeing how they can be utilised more efficiently and applying a disciplined approach to make them more beneficial and productive. You are likely to also find that you emerge with a new perspective on yourself, a greater confidence, and positive expectation that a variety of possibilities of expression and enjoyment in life are waiting for you to grasp with the feeling of a life being renewed.

URANUS TRANSITING 3RD HOUSE

The nature of this phase lies in the struggle between the new and the old, an age-old conflict inherent in life and nature. It is the forming of the 'new order' which is seeking to take its place and role as the dominant factor in your life now. This will involve the battleground of decision, as you prove either that you can break-through in recreating a new, more suitable life, or that you are unable to overthrow existing fixed patterns within your self or external circumstances. You will be attempting to integrate all those new impulses of personal intention/purpose and applying your abilities to make your objectives real.

The struggle is the fact that the old is often inadequate to successfully incorporate the new, and that attempts to modify and adapt the old forms, structures and habit patterns are often failures. Sometimes successful 'grafts' can be made, but there must also be the personal willingness to undergo more radical change in order to make the successful transition. The issue is whether the old order will prove to have too much inertia and restrictive energy preventing growth, or if you are prepared to co-operate with the stimulating vitality of the new incoming energy which is searching for new ways to express its quality of renewal.

Ideally, the vice-like grip of the old has to be broken, and radical changes, either self-created or imposed upon you, are likely. Probably a further modification of your attitudes and values will be required, and it is quite possible that a physical change in your environment may be needed to create a space for the new impulse to emerge victorious. As part of this inner conflict you should receive insight into your own personality and nature, as you directly experience aspects of the multi-faceted 'I' contradicting and co-existing. You need to find ways of resolving such conflicts, so that your energy can be released and freed to move towards your clear direction and purpose. Crises are likely to be created as you struggle to demonstrate your new approach and objectives, and you may experience difficulties again in the effort of communicating these within close relationships. This is partly due to the fact that you are still in the process of coming to terms with and understanding these inner changes in yourself, and the act of defining them and your purposes to others may present problems. However, these challenges are necessary, and serve as a testing ground for you to determine if your intentions are ultimately practical or not and if you are succeeding in expressing the 'new you' in a comprehensible manner. Ideally, you will emerge from this transit having adapted more successfully and fully to these inner changes, and feeling more secure in yourself and in the direction that you have chosen to take.

Uranus transiting 4th House

The unsettling disturbing influence of Uranus will become prominent during this phase, and you are likely to experience your foundations in life being drastically shaken by its impact. These will include your physical, emotional and mental 'roots'. Certain changes in your home pattern are indicated, where the Uranian energy will act as a trend towards undermining any existing security. Your perception of a stable home life is likely to change due to this undermining, and potentially many of your attitudes to life and your reflection of social values can be fundamentally altered.

The Uranian influence will make you question those assumptions upon which you have based your life foundations; what do you need for that sense of security? What is a real home for you? What have you worked towards creating for yourself and others etc? Uranus will make the ground beneath your feet shake - like an earthquake - eroding that reliance and feeling of security and predictability of the known established order.

The most likely areas which will act as focal points for this impulse will be related to work, family losses, family conflicts, belief or ideological structures. Certainly you will be faced with the arising of doubts and questions related to the concepts and realities of 'home and security', and it is likely that any crucial or pivotal events and experiences will occur with a suddenness which tends to leave you basically unprepared. As an extreme worst-case scenario, your whole established life style could suddenly collapse around you, or changes occur which are out of your hands and irrevocable as decisions are made by others, thus leaving you initially impotent and out of control.

Obviously, it will be a challenging period, and much will depend upon how you respond and react. The main point of this impulse is to bring about a redirection within you, to transform any reliance upon external supports for security (work, home, family), towards a desire to discover an inner security and stability; and where you become capable of feeling personally secure in your own unique nature, and less dependent upon materialist supports or others.

This may appear to be 'negative' and a phase to be afraid of. But being aware of the potential nature of this trend can help you to be prepared for it, and should enable you to see clearly what is happening in your life and why.

You could pre-empt part of any negative impact by already looking at those areas of your life, possibly changing some aspects voluntarily. Generally, the strength of the impact of any transit corresponds to whatever is needed for that individual to grow and become more aware, and these transpersonal energies are designed to create a positive individual and collective progression, even though in the short-term their impact can be perceived as quite traumatic in a personal sense. The key is to use them positively through co-operation for your own benefit, and not to fall prey to any evasive unconsciousness reaction and attempted flight away from them. Do that and their destructive quality will be more apparent.

URANUS TRANSITING 5TH HOUSE

This phase is dependent upon the 'success' of your passing through the 4th house transit, and the degree to which you have 're-centred' yourself through working with that abrasive phase.

You will be primarily concerned with forms of creative self-expression. This can be creative activity in a variety of ways, but will be necessary as you attempt to create in a way which develops your sense of relating to others. It may be aimed towards social applications and productivity, possibly reflecting certain of your personal ideals, although this is not essential.

Your creativity, irrespective of to which purpose it is applied, will be motivated by the impulse to enhance and develop your own nature. Whilst you will attempt to be original in your creations, your main personal interest lies in these attitudes 'What can I get out of it?', 'How can this make me feel better, happier, more fulfilled?'. Thus you will relate this impulse to your own unique needs, and any benefits in a broader social sense are viewed as an added bonus.

In some ways, this involves a test of your 'purity of motive'. This does not imply that you should be unselfish and create only for the betterment of others, but indicates that the underlying purpose requires the 'motive' to be a distinct expression of what you are as an individual who is attempting to fulfil a personal destiny of potential. All movement in life towards achieving this state increases the sense of meaning, purpose and fulfillment. Your creative ideas are likely to suddenly strike you as inspirational, and offer a definite image of what you are being asked to create; actually doing so will be the real difficult task.

You will realise that you are outgrowing several old patterns of self, old attitudes and values, and this is likely to lead you towards actively searching for new avenues of life to explore. There may be a feeling of social and personal insecurity, especially if you are restricting and blocking the impulse of creative expression.

The point of this impulse is to recreate parts of yourself, to find new ways of creative relations with others which are dynamic and stimulating, and which encourage you to have a faith in allowing yourself to be more yourself.

Casual relationships are also likely to develop more at this time, which can offer opportunities for a wider scope in personal expression, experience and experimentation, as well as looking to enjoy the pleasures of life in a more insistent manner than before. You may discover additional inspiration from involvements with children, whose more liberated free attitudes towards play and creativity can stimulate a parallel response from you. Education may also attract, as you may require additional training in order for you to create more effectively.

Creativity can take a number of forms, from creating a family, to a process of personal re-creation, artistic forms, scientific or engineering; virtually every aspect of life can be enhanced and explored as a creative expression.

URANUS TRANSITING 6TH HOUSE

During this phase, you are likely to experience a personal crisis, a turning point in your life. This will arise either spontaneously from within reflecting personal discontent, or equally could be imposed upon you by external circumstances.

This process will tend to make you more introspective than previously, as you try to progress beyond those dominating tendencies of personal inertia, limitations and critical self-judgement.

It is a time of readjustment, where you realise that what you do, feel and think does not really match an ideal level of behaviour, personal achievement and success that you have created within. This leads to facing any past failures, and will enhance the process of discontent and inner crisis that will result from such comparisons and questioning. Uranus will act as a stimulating challenge encouraging you to make more effort and progress in achieving your ideals and objectives.

You are likely to realise that your creativity and self expression could be greater if more energy was consciously applied in that direction, and that potentially you could achieve much more in life if you made the effort. This will require you to look again at your life to see what it is that you really want to do with it, realistically evaluating those areas which you can change or where you can exploit your talents fully and thus improve the overall quality of life. In any life, there are many ways in which enjoyment can be deepened, ways to take advantage of those individual talents for satisfaction or profit, new ways to enrich and appreciate life.

The crucial issue is how do you respond to this discontent? What is the quality of your response to the awareness of lack or failure? Crisis is always an opportunity for personal growth, and provided that you do not passively accept any lack as being permanent, with nothing that you can do to change it, the potential is there for you to make long-lasting improvements. But this depends upon clear choice and the application of will. Many lives are ruined by passive acceptance, drained of vitality and enjoyment by an individual inability to reshape unsatisfactory lifestyles.

You should deliberately seek out new techniques, approaches, attitudes and values towards life, which can enable you to fulfil your potential and successfully meet the challenges of this crisis; try not to evade it, because that way only results in self-defeat, but instead try to confront it head on.

There is much suffering and discontent in life, most of which is avoidable if people choose to seriously apply themselves to resolving personal conflicts. Strangely enough, people often seem unaware of their own capacity to change and to heal themselves, because that is a reflection of the dominating social attitude and conditioning.

Conflict is just an expression of an aspect where something is out of harmony and balance in that person or society. In most cases it need not exist, if that person or society is sincere about wanting to be rid of such problems. Many ways currently exist to promote inner health and personal freedom, and you may find that by exploring these certain keys for transformation are discovered. Have the faith that there is a meaning to this discontent and a resolution of it, and have the patience and endurance to see it through. One direction that may be worth looking towards is possibly some form of service to benefit the wider community (and there are a multitude of ways), which could help to clarify and channel your self preoccupations in a positive manner. Possibly changes may occur in your working life which are part of this ongoing pattern, which will have an influence upon your choices at this time. Illness could also occur, possibly as a result of your inner state, and may be 'intended' to create a space in your activities where you can bring about inner change through necessity; but remember that if this does happen, the intention is to create a positive result for you which will lighten your life.

URANUS TRANSITING 7TH HOUSE

At this time, stimulation by Uranus will cause a focus to be placed upon your relationships. It is likely that they will become somewhat unsettled and difficult to predict, especially as the impulse is to become free from the limitations of the established patterns of behaviour within relationships.

You may experience sudden unexpected situations which cause some form of shock or emotional reaction which will condition your behaviour at that time and influence future responses and relationships. Such emotions are likely to be quite powerful and passionate, possibly inspiring, but will certainly make their mark upon you. You may be surprised at their power and impact, and they are likely to high-light any inadequacies in your conception of what your chosen lifestyle should be like. The effects will be disruptive and disturbing.

In this area of your life Uranus is stimulating change, trying to possessions', seeing how they can be utilised more efficiently, and lead you towards a new way of experiencing relationships, so that more depth, meaning and transformatory power is present. This will create the context where you will find that few of your established habit patterns within relationships can remain static or stable under the power of this Uranian influence.

Your attitudes towards personal relations will come under scrutiny, your personal values will be questioned, desires and needs may have to be re-evaluated, and the depth of commitment may be challenged. Objective or external feedback about your actions in relationship is likely, and if that is perceptive and honest, then that can cause a potentially disturbing view of yourself, depending upon your own degree of honesty and perception.

Precisely what will trigger off this phase of enquiry is difficult to say, as there can be several contributory reasons. It often happens in relationships that several lines of habitual response patterns develop, and these circumscribe the range of the interpersonal contact. In an intimate relationship, these operate on several levels, and boundary lines become established and transgressions are penalised by the offended party. These can be trivial or serious boundaries, but each expects the other to conform to these perhaps unspoken demarcation lines, which are 'the terms and conditions of the continuance of the relationship', and these may well be at risk or fluctuate during this phase. In many ways, this can be a positive impact because over time, the vitality of a partnership often tends to diminish until it can cease to satisfy, and more effort and freshness may need to be injected in to revitalise the relationship. Tendencies to over-possessiveness and dominance can occur which create problems; assumptions of 'nothing changing' can develop, creating a situation where a lack of awareness by each partner leads to eventual conflict, as one changes and the other remains static at that time, when different life cycles clash; or desires for 'more' in life lead to friction, or interests and preoccupations begin to diverge.

These aspects of relationship change can occur to yourself or any partner, and they are inevitable. The rosy glow at the start of a marriage or intimate relationship always fades away (to some degree), and the inner patterns of individual development impose their functions upon the partners. It may be you who becomes the instigator of the impulse for radical change, a disturbing influence who is passing through a crucial process of questioning; or you could find that the initial stimulus emanates from others who begin to behave in ways that disturb your settled equilibrium, and which throw you into a state of questioning or confusion.

Depending upon the degree of inner adjustment that is 're-quired' within you, will be the strength of the impact upon your life of this transit. Obviously the more awareness that you can bring to all of your relationships the better, and so needing less forced change. Be prepared for these tendencies to occur during this phase, and do not avoid the process but co-operate with this impulse. Its intention is to make your experience of personal relations more fulfilling and meaningful, so it should not be viewed negatively but seen as an opportunity to become a little wiser and to create the condition where within yourself, you are capable of enjoying life more, and in so doing share this with others.

URANUS TRANSITING 8TH HOUSE

The 8th house will be the testing ground for the results of your experiences and changes which you have undergone so far in this cycle. In particular, you will be looking to see what pragmatic and concrete results you have achieved. They may be of a positive nature, enhancing the beneficial effects of this process, personally, socially and materially, if you have successfully ridden the energy of change, and have co-operated with its revolutionary influence. Or you may have to see your failures more clearly, if through your resistance and lack of commitment the energy of change has been repulsed and the potential for renewal has been aborted.

For now, the time has passed to be absorbed with dreams and wishes for your life. The emphasis has been transferred to that of a practical demonstration and expression of your current ideals through your own nature, and in relationships or business life. The time that you have previously spent in developing theories and ideals is to be tested through applying them in the fires of the real world.

It is the opportunity for you to embody more fully your dreams and ideals; this may require a deeper conscious fusing with your life, attitudes and values, as you have to live them out, and they should not be mere cosy illusions that you fill your mind with, pretending that you are committed to them. The point of this is that in action you discover the impact, influence, power and value of these personal ideals released into real life, so that you can see if it is easy to apply them consistently, to observe their effect, and to note how they transform yourself or what questions they may stimulate.

In practise, any attempt to reflect what one believes – as fully as possible – is always extremely difficult. The tendency is to compromise for the sake of expediency. This can eventually lead – if continued – to giving mere lip-service to ideals and beliefs, and will create entrenched inner conflicts and a sense of failure. It is a common state, especially amongst those who give superficial allegiance to ideals and beliefs. The main value of an ideal is as a goal towards which a person is encouraged to aim, thus moving beyond many of their initial limitations, and coming to express their unique potential.

It may be that you experience the apparent failure of your ideals and beliefs when confronted by reality, or find yourself criticised or rejected by others for a particular stand or position that you choose to take. To some degree such responses should be expected. If your ideals are obviously inadequate, impractical or too far-reaching for the present time, then this fact should be faced. Many visionary social ideals take much more than a lifetime to make any discernible progress, especially the epochal visions emanating from the transpersonal planets of Uranus, Neptune and Pluto. However, you may find that, by making certain re-evaluations and adjusting your expectations, some success can be obtained and some progress made (especially if your ideals are orientated towards social change).

Disillusionment is the constant companion of the ideal, yet even disillusionment can lead to the ideal being made more realistic and achievable. People often overreach themselves with the power of ideals, and can lose the positive impulse which leads them in such a direction. If your deepest ideals and beliefs are rejected by those most closely involved with you, this can be extremely painful. It may be that you have not adapted to the reality of the world or taken the needs of others into sufficient consideration. You will have to make a hard personal choice as to what to do, although it is usually best to follow your own path wherever it leads; even if your choice is 'wrong' you can learn much of value. Essentially, the hidden focus is upon the interaction between yourself and society, and your ideals should reflect this relationship. You should not over-emphasise either yourself or the collective, because this would be unbalancing. You are attempting to make yourself a channel of change aiming at the eventual reconstruction of harmony.

URANUS TRANSITING 9TH HOUSE

Continuing from the challenge of the 8th house transit, and the interaction between your ideals and society, this phase focuses on the need to consider your relationships in their context and role as providers of meaning in your life. The need for meaning and purpose is fundamental to a fulfilling human life, and as such it contributes a 'spiritual food' parallel to the physical needs for survival.

You are likely to review the results of your efforts of the previous transit, to determine the degree of success that you actually achieved. As usual with a Uranian transit, its entrance into a new house often acts as a trigger to transmit several new and potentially unsettling thoughts, concepts or experiences into your life. There are few periods of rest and tranquillity under the Uranian influence, as its restless spirit is perpetually searching and enquiring the way forward. Stagnation or static passivity is not allowed.

It is a time to devote effort towards greater understanding, as usual stimulated by those unsettling doubts arising within you which lead to questioning. Whilst initially disturbing, this can act as a great clarifier and bringer of light.

You will consider the nature and role of relationships in your life, asking how and why they have ultimately contributed to the sort of results you have experienced, examining what could be the under-lying purpose and value of these relationships. This involves determining the perspective from which you are judging and evaluating them, and how self-orientated this perception is. How do your closest intimates judge your role in them? You have to ask whether your relationships are satisfying and fulfilling for all the participants, whether they are beneficial and liberating or person-ally restrictive.

These can be difficult questions to handle, and obviously you will formulate your own personal questions, but it is better that you take the time to allow answers and an understanding of this process to form itself within you. Immediate answers – especially poten-tially negative ones – can become transformed if you allow time to reveal what it is that you are looking for, and then to discover if it is possible to uncover it within present relationships. Often, taking a new approach and attitude can stimulate great changes, revital-ising partnerships and unveiling latent aspects of the relationship that had no space to emerge into being whilst under the constraints of those particular habit patterns that were obviously mutually developed.

Often in life, people almost automatically conform with society and collective purposes, and questioning is often discouraged in preference to an adherence to established social traditions and attitudes. In some ways, this can be effective if everything is proceeding fine with a life, but if crises occur and the established pattern is shattered, people often become lost as they have never been taught to understand their own nature and the natural processes of life; or how to question in order to receive inner insight and understanding, and eventually inner guidance for their life-direction.

All self-understanding is beneficial. It creates a context for personal motivation and direction which is based upon your own needs, desires and unique individuality, enhancing enjoyment as your life becomes more self-controlled, meaningful and purposeful.

URANUS TRANSITING 10TH HOUSE

This phase is focused upon the social fruits of your exploration of your unique individuality and your efforts to express it in the world. The possibility is that your sphere of social influence will begin to expand. Are you ready for that?

It is the development and consummation of the process which commenced at the start of this Uranus cycle, and involves the concepts of social function and power, the integration of the individual into the surrounding larger community or society.

This involves the relationship between self and society, the intermingling of personal and social needs for mutual benefit, and the influence that powerful and dominating personalities can have upon the malleable social fabric of a nation or a locality. The right approach to this leads far beyond purely personal interests, into social responsibility.

It is probable that you will emerge into a higher social profile than previously, a new or revised role that leads to a greater interaction with others offering the potential of some degree of social influence. This will be a challenge for you, requiring considerable application of will and ambition in order to succeed, plus a clear intention of your purpose in such a position.

Many people have problems with the assumption of power and influence. It is a responsibility, and as such needs to be handled with the maximum awareness and social conscience, especially where decisions made can have an impact on the well-being and lives of others. Power is more often abused than rightly used, and often serves to stimulate those seeds of personal exaltation and the consciousness of separateness rather than creating unity and harmony through co-operation.

Through these more socially orientated activities, you will need to observe the degree to which you are capable of expressing your individual nature in a meaningful way. You will have to ask yourself if the position to which you have attained is what you intended, and if it is fulfilling for you. If it is, then you have the possession of the key that will open the door to greater meaning and purpose in your life. If it does not satisfy, then you need to explore the reasons why your vision went wrong, or which unsuitable choices were made, or where your lack of self-understanding let you down.

Especially during the early period of this transit, be alert to all opportunities that come your way. Doors of potential will appear and it is up to you to recognise them, grasp the opportunities presented and move through them so that expansion can occur.

URANUS TRANSITING 11TH HOUSE

Uranus and the sign of Aquarius have a natural affinity and resonance to the 11th house, which is associated with concepts of social brotherhood and group consciousness. In distinction to the 5th house, where the creative process is primarily orientated to the individual and reflected as a personal expression, the 11th house variation is directed towards the more transpersonal dimension. Here the individual is perceived more as a channel for those transformatory and revolutionary energies to interpenetrate with this world, and is a function and task that is expected to be performed by the majority of the readers of this book.

Under this influence, you will feel inclined to explore the less charted waters of human existence, to explore spheres of mystery and evocative fascination. The search for newness will again be present, but should be much less disruptive than before. This is because you are coming towards the end of this cycle, and are reaping the rewards of previous efforts.

Much will depend upon your success during the 10th house transit. If your effort to deepen your social participation and influence was effective, then you will feel enthusiastically inspired to direct your creative efforts towards a progressive renewal of society. This is through being involved and active with those visionary, forward-looking movements and groups which aim to create a better life for all, those with probably an ecological and humanistic perspective.

If your experience of the 10th house transit was disappointing and disillusioning, then try to ensure that it does not leave too bitter an after-taste, leading to frustration and aggression. The possibility is that you could turn against society and people, and through frustration allow your ideals and vision to become distorted. Great idealistic success is very rare, yet limited success is always probable, and it is better to make some progress than none at all. You may be tempted to look for forms of escapism to assuage your disillusionment, but to fall under the influences of social drugs and addictive temptations is certainly not the answer to a sense of inner frustration.

From the more positive perspective, you will need to remain open-minded, looking primarily for truth, and you will note that you have little concern for maintaining traditions or assumed social values unelss they are genuinely felt as real and relevant to your life. Your attitude will become more humanitarian, seeing humanity more in terms of a world group and brotherhood/sisterhood, a communal-world family.

It is likely that you will form new and unusual friendships which you find are mentally stimulating and influential, and this can emerge via an association with futurist groups. You will probably look for those unconventional people with whom you feel more affinity and sense of community.

You are likely to move towards a more unconventional and impersonal approach to any marriage or relationships, perhaps as a response to the broader vision that is currently inspiring you. This can lead to problems in feeling tied down to any one single relationship, as you may feel the need and desire to experience a greater degree of independence and freedom at this time.

You will have to be careful not to develop a too irresponsible and impractical set of ideas and ideals towards social change. You may become too mentally stimulated by new ideas that you can lose sight of the fact that people have to apply them and potentially live by them, and that they have to respond positively in order for ideals to become real in the world, and not remain as mind theories.

URANUS TRANSITING 12TH HOUSE

This is the final phase and culmination of this Uranus cycle, which has been devoted to the gradual working through of your creative potential and social involvement.

It is a period concerned with an 'ending' that now faces you, where the underlying motivating impulse of the whole cycle has led you to the point at which you now stand. This revolutionary impulse, responsible for activating and stimulating these changes in your life is no longer vitalised or effective, in fact it is 'dying' and you are proceeding on a course developed from past momentum. You are being prompted to review the results of this cycle, be they relatively successful or relative failures, and to understand the intrinsic meaning and purposeful pattern to them, drawing those conclusions and lessons from them which have emerged over time.

This phase is like a pause in the influence of Uranus upon you, and is designed to enable you to initiate a period of reorientation which is suitable to lead you into a new cycle. This will bring a new impulse, a new direction for you to understand its message and intention.

Once you feel that you have evaluated your conclusions and lessons, then do not spend any more time looking towards the recent past. You have to become prepared to receive the new energy from Uranus, which is likely to be initially present (or hidden) within some experience which will happen quite unexpectedly to you. This experience will hold the seed for the new cycle, and by which you will obviously be heavily conditioned.

In a way, it is like a new gestation leading to birth for you, and will offer new opportunity for your growth and progress. You will have to be willing to undergo future changes, as resistance will not prove to be of any advantage. Always remember that the underlying intention is designed to be positive and beneficial.

Uranus will stimulate a sense of unease and discontent within several aspects of your life. This is to encourage evolutionary change to occur, and where discontent exists there is the indication that improvements can be made to enrich life and to enjoy it to the fullest extent possible; this should be an aim for everyone, to appreciate the rich variety and fullness of life.

Through this planetary method, Uranus also demonstrates that no level of success is final, but represents only one step forward, or that apparent failure is not final either, but only a step away from future success. Fortunately, life is not essentially limiting, unless we limit ourselves, but always offers the potential for a more abundant life to be experienced and enjoyed. It is individual choice that contains the key.

CHAPTER 7

The Esoteric Uranus

URANUS HAS BEEN DESCRIBED as the 'ancient mystery planet of occultism' and until the late eighteenth century was 'hidden' behind Saturn, who is known as the 'Lord of Karma'. The creation myths associated with Uranus, are representations of previous esoteric mystery school teachings concerning the power of mental imaging or visualisation. These reflect the Vedic concepts that the universe is but a dream in the mind of Brahma, a divine fantasy and drama.

In many modern occult schools, there is considerable emphasis placed upon understanding the nature of mind, and being trained to use the mind creatively to build a better world, individually and collectively. Currently we can see a large amount of literature and courses entering the market-place which are designed to ' unleash the powers of your mind'. Whilst it may not be immediately obvious today, such emphasis upon the culture of the mind through using various techniques is relatively modern. The spread of literacy and intellectualism – irrespective of social class – has only occurred in recent history, since the emergence of Uranus; and the esoteric explorations and revelations concerning mind have only been commonly released since the mid nineteenth century.

Uranus is the stimulator of mind, the investigator into the inner spaces of the hidden creative universe. His impact is to rouse us from a focus within instinctual and emotionally based life reactions (as reflected by the potency and activity of the energy chakras below the heart), and to transfer our energies upwards to open and activate latent areas of the mind-brain.

Uranus is the 'Great Awakener', the shock of realisation which shatters the mental barrier of the illusion of separateness, when the 'lower mind drops and the light of the higher mind shines and perceives the real universe'. In esoteric terms which are associated with Eastern and theosophically derived teachings, this is the First Initiation, where the energy rises to its new level of radiance in the heart chakra, and a vision of the unity of humanity and earth is realised. This stage is considered in more detail in *Phoenix Rising*, where the emphasis is placed upon the function and role of Pluto in this evolutionary process. These two transpersonal planets and Neptune merge their complementary energies as a group transformatory influence.

Uranus is the initiator of a new order and structure of life, giving man an understanding of the hidden causal patterns, and amplifying his desire to improve the quality of life by continual renewal. This is the impulse to create better living conditions through the process of civilisation, more effective material forms for our needs, and to integrate those disparate aspects of our nature into an operating unity.

The 'scientific mind' has Uranian characteristics which reflect its role as the Logos Principle. These include impersonality, the capacity for abstract thinking, logic and rationality, decisive clarity, a cold objectivity and a persistent will. The Uranus influence occurs in the need within mind to transmute the fragmentation of acquired knowledge – which commonly occurs today – into a comprehensive synthesis which can reveal greater light and wisdom. The continuing information explosion of recent years can create more confusion and lack of clarity, unless the information is considered within a unifying conceptual framework. The analytical approach to scientific and intellectual disciplines has to begin to coalesce through a conscious process of synthesis, in order to reveal the underlying patterns of meaning and significance.

What this is moving towards is a state described as 'occult consciousness', which is an at-one-ment achieved through an intelligent use of the synthetic quality of mind, which fuses the higher and lower aspects of mind together, in an integration of the 'inner and outer self'.

This is the Uranian aspect of unification between spirit and matter, between the Sky God and the Earth Goddess. It is this that is the sphere of magic, the operating realm of the occultists, and the quest to invoke the immanence of divinity through themselves as sacrificial channels.

Uranus is known as the ruler of the occult path, both reflecting his status as First Father, and his position as the first mystery planet of the transpersonal spaces. Esoterically, he is connected with the supervisory role and function of the Hierophant, who is the official revealer of the sacred mysteries and ceremonies, and initiating priest. It is the high planet of occultism 'for it veils "that which is essential; it hides that which must be discovered, and at the right moment, it transmits knowledge of the hidden mystery." ' He agitates the curiosity of the seeker, so that the will intensifies into a burning fire, which evokes 'the will to be and to know on all planes of manifestation'.*

Dane Rudhyar considers that Uranus is the 'Master of Transformation', and is the creative power of the universal spirit. He identifies the activity of the Uranian energy on the initiate as the stage of the Third Initiation, that of the personal transfiguration, corresponding to the light which the disciples saw shining from and through Christ as he was attended by the two ancient prophets. The transfigured individual then becomes a focal point for the release of the power of the universal mind, thus fusing spirit and matter.

Esoterically, the activity of Uranus is only consciously registered at an advanced stage of development on the path. This is when the conscious illumined disciple through an act of will arouses the chakra at the base of the spinal channel, and deliberately draws up the kundalini fire. As the disciple is focused in the head centres, he is able to control and direct the fiery energies correctly and safely in his occult work. As Hierophant, Uranus supervises the action of the solar angel (soul) upon the personality of the aspirant, up to the Third Initiation. The full impact of the electrical nature of Uranus is experienced during the later stages of the path, when the initiated soul is led to the burning ground where the Fifth Initiation occurs; the release into Masterhood and the escape from the 'Wheel of Life' is achieved under the energies of Uranus and Jupiter.

The wisdom teachings of the trans-Himalayan school (as transmitted through Alice Bailey) suggest that Uranus is the exoteric ruler of Aquarius, the esoteric ruler of Libra, and is exalted in Scorpio. This suggests that the real purpose of the Uranian energy is to create a state of inner balance, so that the mind is raised above the level of conflicting dualism. This is achieved through the fire by friction stimulated by Scorpio–Plutonic intensity, and the experiences associated with the 8th house patterns of life, death, rebirth and resurrection. Harmony can then occur as a result of the resolving of dualistic conflicts.

* Quotes reprinted with permission from Alice A. Bailey, *A Treatise on the Seven Rays, Vol. III, Esoteric Astrology* (Lucis Trust Ltd).

It may also be worth noting that it is the 11th house which is associated with Uranus and group relations, and 11 is the number which is connected to the Initiate. The initiate may appear to be a solitary figure, but the work which he is engaged upon is always related to the progress of the larger group, and the well-being of the whole.

URANUS AND THE 7TH RAY ENERGY

Within the esoteric system of the Seven Rays, Uranus is associated with the 7th Ray. It can be of value to consider the characteristics of this particular energy ray in connection with the vibration of Uranus.

The 7th Ray is identified with ceremonial magic and ritual, organisation and relationship, and is associated with the use and transmission of higher spiritual energies through into the denser planes of the personality and material levels. This is the task of the white magician applying the esoteric science of unification to bring about the fused relationship of spirit and matter, soul, personality and form.

The ultimate intent of this evocation of spiritual energy is to inaugurate a new world order, which is founded upon a spiritual impulse and the aspiration for mental freedom, collective social harmony through a loving understanding of our common humanity, and a physical plane lifestyle that offers full opportunity for creative expression. This 'Ray of Ritualistic Decency' aspires to build the utopian ideal of the 'kingdom of heaven on earth'. Here we can see the correspondences with the astrological and mythological Uranus; the urges for mental freedom and creativity, the universal brotherhood ideal, the priest-hierophant, and the attempts of the god Uranus to create a beautiful idealistic offspring to match his heavenly imagination. The only problem is us, and our slowness in evolving to become capable of manifesting this purpose. But still, Uranus does not let us rest. He shakes us in our sleep-walking, disrupts our habit patterns of unconscious behaviour insisting that we wake to something new, and collaborates with Pluto to destroy our reliance upon the Saturnian, fixed, protective yet binding ring-pass-nots of our personal and social structures. We cannot resist the influence of the transpersonal planets; we can attempt to deny them access, but then that energy will just destroy our barricades, sweeping through our efforts at imposing order and leaving us forced to change and grow in the midst of the chaotic devastation that they can leave in their wake.

It is via the 7th Ray that one of the more direct lines of 1st Ray energy can travel. The impact of the 'Great Destroyer' of the 1st Ray as mediated through Pluto is also transmitted through this connection with Uranus. This is the implication of the exaltation of Uranus in Scorpio, which is ruled by Pluto. The merging of Uranus and Pluto in this work releases the imprisoned life force into a rebirth, where the old inhibiting forms, ways of living, culture and civilisation are either destroyed or heavily modified. The chaos which is the initial result of a 1st Ray impact is then reorganised by the 7th Ray, which re-establishes a new order and rhythm suitable for the next step in creative expression.

Certain results of 7th Ray activity can be noted in contemporary times. These are based on two occult axioms that reflect the embryonic creation of magical formulas which are designed to effect change on the planes of human consciousness and physical plane activity. These formulas emerge from the hermetic concept of 'As above, so below', which is a clear definition of the unificatory paradigm that is embodied by the 7th Ray. The axioms are 'Energy follows thought' and 'Right motive creates right action and right forms'. Anyone who is working with the 7th Ray will recognise these as precise guidelines that they are attempting to follow in their creative and relating work. Learning the laws of building effective thought-forms and vitalising them by the applied energy of will is starting to become common knowledge, and in a variety of ways is experimented with by all occultists, with varying degrees of success. Yet it will prove to be this key to using our minds (under spiritual impression) that will unlock the door to mankind's future evolution in the Aquarian Age and beyond. Implicit in the second axiom of 'Right motive creates right action and right forms' is the fact that this power can be misused through wrong motives; the magical sword is always 'double-edged'.

One clear expression of applying this 7th Ray energy, is the development of influencing the mass mind through advertising and the creation of political slogans, or entertainer's 'catch phrases'. Whilst in some ways, this is a debasement of the energy, we can recognise how effective this technique of creating a 'magical word formula' can be. We can probably remember several examples of the use by entertainers, and modern politics strives to create succinct word syntheses of impressions that it wants to transmit to the electorate. Subliminal techniques of positive affirmations on

'New Age Music' tapes can bear witness to the almost hypnotic effect of our rediscovery of the mantric science of the power in words. Eventually, we will rediscover the ancient knowledge of the magical use of words of power.

Associated with the activity of Uranus is 'radiatory activity'. We can see the signs of this in the explosion of new ideas, the increase in the rate of the information curve, mental activity (radiation and psychic telepathy); and the unlocking of radiatory heat and energy within matter, and the radioactivity of uranium.

Through the scientific investigation penetrating into the atomic and subatomic worlds of matter, we have seen the birth during this century of a new dimension of science. This is a breaking free of the impasse which had been reached when operating from a materialistic perception of reality. The new step forward involves the transferring of the focus of investigation into the realms of the intangible and subjective universe. Through exploring the inner spaces of matter, we can correspondingly explore the inner spaces of the human psyche, where the scientist can no longer objectively examine 'out there', but also has to examine himself to determine the influence of his subjective participation in his experiments. Quantum physics and mechanics is delving into this metaphysical world, where the distinctions between subject and object dissolve, and which appears similar to the oneness experience of the initiate or mystic.

The relationship between Uranus and Sky God and Gaia the Earth Mother is reflected again in the association of 7th Ray relatedness. This involves the basic polarity of positive and negative natural processes of physical plane procreation. The issue of sexual relationships is an old one, with discord dating back even to Uranus and Gaia! Whilst most adults have some kind of sexual life, there is still some disquiet concerning our understanding and hidden inner relationship to sex. Society has ambiguous attitudes, through morals, religion, family structures, sexual taboos, and concepts of perversions; and similarly individuals often have some degree of inner confusion. Our modern Western world expresses most of these aspects relatively openly, and divorces and homosexuality are facts of contemporary life. As we have seen, Uranus is often associated with sexual novelty, promiscuousness, sexual eccentricity or perversion, and with homosexuality. But I think that this is a passing and temporary phase, where these aspects of the variety of human sexuality are coming to the surface prior to being acknowledged, understood and accepted. Partly, it is a problem due to human responsiveness to the Uranian energy, whereby the individual is only capable of an erratic response which churns the depths but is often not sufficient to transform cleanly and decisively.

Eventually, as the potency of the Uranus-7th Ray energies intensifies, and the burning grounds of change are traversed, the quality of relatedness will move to the forefront of consciousness, and a new inclusive attitude and understanding of the mystery of sexual polarity will emerge. Signs of this are being displayed in existing concepts of androgyny, which is being promoted as a mental image of inner balance. Jungian psychology indicates the need for the integration of the qualities of the opposite sex within the individual consciousness, through entering into relationship with the archetypes of the anima and animus (see *Phoenix Rising* for further details). What is essential is for a new relationship between the positive and negative poles of life, the heavens and the earth, in order for a planetary integration of wholeness to occur.

Being children of Gaia, we have to welcome the return of our first father back into our lives, serve to mediate between Gaia and Uranus, and raise our body and minds of matter to grasp the spiritual hand that Uranus is offering to us. Through our evolution, Gaia and Uranus can embrace again.

CHAPTER 8

Uranus and the Impulse of the Aquarian Age

A NEW ASTROLOGICAL AGE indicates the awakening of previously dormant aspects of the human being, slowly unfolding the potential of latent spirituality within the collective psyche as a whole. The transition to a new age is like the ticking of an evolutionary clock, which is a monitoring factor in the slow progression into global awareness of humanity. As the founders of religions like Christ and Buddha demonstrate, individual progress can be made much more quickly, and these become the seeding forefathers of future development, but for the majority, growth can be laboriously slow, difficult and erratic.

These new zodiacal ages occur every 2,160 years approximately (as a twelve-fold division of a total cycle of 25,900 years). We do not really know when each of the cyclic ages commences, or how much of an overlap between signs is required for a clear transition. As Uranus is the first of the modern planets to be discovered, symbolising the threshold to the transpersonal planets, it could be considered that the transition into the Aquarian Age commenced at its discovery, especially as Uranus is the co-ruler of Aquarius with Saturn.

Previous cyclic phases of the total precession have been the Age of Taurus the Bull, where the more physical animal nature of man was more dominant and expressive; the Age of Aries the Ram, symbolised by the Old Testament sacrifice of the lamb, where the human transition is from the dominant physical nature towards that of human feelings and emotions, closer family and tribal ties of community; and the Age of Pisces the Fishes, where the mind of man awakens, and the nature of dualistic conflicts and perceptions of reality begin to dominate. The essential point of the dawning

Aquarian Age is to resolve these dualities and separatist notions through moving beyond the lower analytical mind and contacting that point where the awareness of unity is constantly realised; some traditions call this the soul, the inner divinity, the godhead within.

Uranus and Saturn are co-rulers of Aquarius. As we have already considered, this polarity of energy interchanges is a vitalising force in the evolutionary struggle. Yet as planetary rulers, they also indicate that the glorious vision of Aquarius will not be achieved overnight, and that the conflict of past and future magnetic attractions (similar to the Moon's Nodes) within the individual and society will be difficult to resolve without suffering. They also act as counterbalances between too rapid a movement forward, or an insistence on denying change; arguably, they present the safest passage onward that can be achieved by humanity, especially when considering the depth of changes which are envisaged. These include even genetic development or mutations within the species, the awakening of areas of the brain, as well as collective social adjustments and planetary changes. In an extremely complex life web on Earth, regulation and development needs to be carefully overseen by the planetary consciousness of Gaia. The natural balances are fragile, and through ignorance, humanity is now seriously affecting them. We need to become wiser in order to survive in a world of indterependence.

The vision of right human relationships as impulsed by the Uranus archetype is the rallying call of the French Revolution, 'Liberty, Equality and Fraternity!' This remains as the foundation of the Aquarian ideal of group consciousness and universal brotherhood, and is a utopian concept, but one that is essential for humanity to strive towards. Since that first Uranian declaration, the Western world has been plunged into rapid change and crisis, both through its economic and industrial developments and through fundamental changes in its internal social structures of democracy and social improvements. It is a combination of the mind aspect becoming more socially prominent, and the resulting application of intelligence to raise the quality of life of society, as well as an unfolding of the compassionate heart. These are great milestones, even though we often lose sight of them through our preoccupations with our individual lives and struggles. Yet the pressures of such developments have also led to 'explosions' of tensions and attempts to restore old patterns of behaviour; the World Wars are evidence of collective social breakdowns, phases of a gradual transition. We stand on the brink of a further stage of this process now; as we face the next millennium and the Aquarian vision clarifies, we need to be sure what we are doing and where we are going in the light of an interdependent world.

The symbol of Aquarius is the Waterbearer, the esoteric keynote is 'Water of Life am I, poured forth for thirsty men', and the astrological glyph suggests the images of rippling waves, the wind–air movement, and serpents of wisdom. The urn that the bearer carries on his shoulder is the pitcher aligned with the 'vast spiritual reservoir in which we live and move and have our being', the spiritual world of energies and forces of universal life and consciousness. Yet this world which often appears in the form of water symbols and images is really a world of mind interpreting messages from a hidden reality; from these 'seas of mind' we contact an overflowing realm of fecundity, permanently pregnant and giving birth to ideas which will find root somewhere in the universe.

The Western Mystery School image of the Grail reflects this inner reality. We are encouraged to discover our own personal grail, experience the results of an individual quest to contact the soul; in so doing, we find that the next step involves working with the national racial grail, and then service to the planetary grail. The Grail is a multi-dimensional, multi-levelled archetypal symbol, reflecting myriad facets to each who succeed in their approach, and is a never-ending chalice of inspiration. The 'Grail Knights' are those who have reached the point of an intellectual understanding of the brotherhood vision, and have moved beyond and deeper into the experiencing of universality through the opened intuitive mind. Currently, we are seeing the growing appeal of this symbolic imagery into the mind of man, as the Waterbearer grows more real and potent in the collective psyche. A symbol is, after all, a visible external form and impression of a hidden inner reality, and the underlying astrological images help to form the spiritual symbols of meaning and direction for that age.

What is this Aquarian Grail that Uranus is so concerned with promoting? What is the point of Uranus disrupting the individual and collective life?

Uranus and crisis move together hand in hand, yet crisis is just a phase in a pattern of growth, whereby new energies are released to stimulate individual or collective tranformation. What these lead to are points of decision and choice, 'fated arrival/destination points', where resolution or attempts at denial and refusals to confront may be taken. The individual or society is faced with those crystallised attitude patterns that need to be broken or transcended in order to become free of a dangerous impasse that has been sequentially created by following those patterns. Each pattern of expression has its time; initially it can be positive in nature, but past a certain stage, its effects become increasingly negative. Uranus tries to inspire the person to move beyond purely individual concerns and perceptions of life, so that a collective function of revealing meaning and purpose can also be achieved. This is the transpersonal life of a deeper relationship between the individual evolution and collective progress, which in itself requires the individual to forge an independent path of self-exploration and enquiry often against social traditions and belief structures. It is only through the act of ongoing questioning that new insights can be received, and through being open to different answers.

Uranus helps to blast open that door to the collective unconscious mind, helping to release those more universally applicable values and interpretations of life. It forces us to realise and accept that, in a changing world, we too are being asked to change as a process of adaptation. Looking backwards into a golden past is not the style of Uranus; looking forwards into a golden future is.

The future direction is indicated in the polarity of the Aquarius–Leo axis; in Leo, the individual expresses the attitude of standing at the centre of the universe through a separating mental filter, yet in Aquarius this is transformed and exalted into a group consciousness of humanity. Instead of a personal creativity for self-advancement, it becomes creativity as service for the benefit of all. The key message in this progression is that of conscious relationship.

The Aquarian Age is the world birth of a new science of relationships, a realisation of interdependence and intrinsic unity. In each of the modern branches of science, as well as in the emerging new disciplines, this is the realm of life that is acting as a renewing area of exploration. Old scientific assumptions and theories of reality are either being deposed or redefined. The developing gap between current knowledge and the structures and attitudes of world societies needs to be narrowed as soon as possible.

With the associations between Uranus, Aquarius, Air and the 11th house, it is the level of mind that is being highly stimulated. In the modern West, it is intellect that has been elevated into a dominant position, and its curiosity to probe into the mysteries of nature has led it to a point where in order to understand more, it has to go beyond its analytical approach. This quantum leap involves moving from a false position of objective observer, into a subjective experience of the realms of energy and mind that we exist within, and a dissolution of the beliefs of dualism through that inner knowing of conscious relationship to the universe.

This growing transfer of perception is evidenced in the explorations of the new physics, transpersonal psychology, biological morphic resonance theories, parapsychology, metaphysics and alternative health therapies – all of which are founded on concepts of holism or intrinsic relationships of the total energy network.

This is why much of the initial spearhead of the Uranus/ Aquarius impulse is found operating through that 11th sign and house, where scientists, occultists, political reformers and social revolutionaries derive their inspiration. It is this group that is channelling through the new visionary patterns, and receiving the guiding intuitions for appropriate directions to explore. Part of the purpose of Aquarius is to enhance communication through mental faculties, especially those of speech and writing, and logic and rational expression; this will expand to include more intuitional aspects, especially if performing the function of transmitting 'messages from the Gaia consciousness'.

As a symbol is an external form reflecting an inner reality, the signs of intrinsic relationship are already part of the modern world. Satellites and electronic communications networks are a vital aspect, and function like a collective nervous system, relaying world information around the globe. These parallel the human brain, where information is received and transmitted through electrical charges. The human mind has been 'extended' through the use of computers, which can process data more efficiently, effectively and quickly, and through the development of robotics can perform such factory tasks as car production. Governments, businesses and the media all rely on this global nerve network of communications operating properly. The world money markets are advanced users of the Aquarian/7th Ray impulse, where the energies of money are manipulated without objective form through computer transactions, for the benefit and operation of international business organisations. We are building a global brain from electronic signals; we are mimicking an existing situation within the ecological Gaia.

Yet the sheer flood of information and data flowing across the world can lead to a 'neural overburdening'. There is an information explosion occurring with accelerating speed which is moving even

faster than social changes. This parallels the intensification of life
that is experienced in the individual as a result of Uranus activity,
and is a rushing towards crisis or fate, prior to a breakdown or
transformation of the person or social system.

Social and individual change are intertwined; what is required
is a personal and collective metamorphosis, a reorganisation of
fragmented aspects into a cohesive pattern of relationship and
holistic vision. This is the Aquarian Grail symbol, from which
pours the highest ideal of good, and embodies a new step for
humanity, revealing a new facet of the 'mystery of God'. The
friction between an attempted union of opposites can now be
resolved. As Uranus comes closer again, responding to the needs of
Gaia, we can act as mediators for their relationship. As offspring of
their first progeny, we partake of their nature, and have the work
of fusing the physical and spiritual together in balance and harmony. Individually and collectively we have to resolve duality into
unity, we are asked to make the vision of Uranus real, and not just
an ideal existing solely within mind.

Similar to the concepts of a social or world hologram, where the
whole is reflected in its totality by each of its individual parts, a new
form of 'social collectivism' will emerge as a fusing of the essential
impulses behind the political attitudes of democracy and Communism. This will be a balance between individual and collective
rights, founded on a shared group purpose and direction, similar to
that currently experimented within intentional communities like
Findhorn, where the focus is a universal family symbol. Such an
approach will be firmly rooted in the attitude of responsibility for
personal and social choices, a belief that we have the choice of
creating our society according to our vision, and transforming it too
whenever the need for re-creation emerges. The image of the
magician as conscious manipulator of energies in building an ideal
world reflects both the 7th Ray and the Tarot trump, which is why
at this point in evolution, it is undergoing such a remarkable
renaissance as a power symbol.

During the first stage of the Aquarian Age, the role of Saturn will
dominate, where there will be political upheavals reflecting the
deep underlying social changes happening. New structures, ideals
and social expressions will struggle with the existing order for
existence, and the polarisation between the past and future is the
battleground. By the second stage, when much of this will have
been resolved in favour of the incoming impulse, the orientation
will move towards a socially positive education to develop mental

illumination and group consciousness of global interdependence. This will be the result of the stimulating and awakening of the compassionate heart to the unnecessary suffering of people in the world. The time-scale for such developments depends upon our acceptance and application of the brotherhood ideal.

The scale of this world transformation is potentially vast. It involves the transcending of a perception of life that is basically materialistic into one that perceives the universe as a sea of mind, conscious energies and forces in eternal interplay. It is a subversion of the dominance of the Saturn–Gaia supremacy, to one where Uranus is restored to his spiritual position, although this time hopefully in harmony with Gaia. Such progress should be achieved by the end of the Aquarian Age, as the mental barriers fragmenting the vision of unity are broken, and the mind is capable of holistic thought.

Through exploring the face of nature and the human being, we are tearing away the veils of ignorance. Entering the holy of holies we strip away the illusions of Gaia and self, only to rediscover the reality that at the heart of both the religious and scientific impulse exists a concealed Deity. At this point in evolution, it is the First Father, Uranus whom we expose in the light.

... To Evolution

IT IS INTERESTING TO OBSERVE that even the astronomical physical Uranus has no respect for the established pattern of planetary rotation in our solar system. Uranus rotates in a radically different direction, having its polar axes in an east–west position, rather than the more common north–south axis, and so to the observer from Earth appears to rotate on its belly. Even in this way, Uranus demonstrates that there can be other equally valid ways to be, that life does not have to be orthodox and conform to the majority pattern, and that difference, uniqueness and eccentricity is a great contribution to the variety of life. It is a pointer to the realisation that the transcendent creator has an infinite imagination, the likes of which we can barely conceive.

Every one of us experiences the struggle between the Saturn and Uranus energies. Humanity is torn between trying to impose meaning and order on a changing, shifting world, through the attempt to feel secure, stable and in control, and the radical and revitalising radical impulses of Uranus. Human history is formed by the clash between those who respond to each of these energies.

In essence, Uranus is not just a revolutionary opposing a powerful establishment seeking to protect an unchanging status quo, but is truly an *evolutionary spirit* leading and inspiring us to actualise greater dreams and visions. As a breaker of limitations, Uranus opens us to the new worlds that we have still to explore, as we progress ever higher on the spiral of life. At present, we recognise Uranus in the guise of a revolutionary spirit – which to some is a fashionable image – but the next step in the development of our understanding of Uranus is to perceive him as an inspirational god, the evolutionary spirit of the First Father.

Uranus is an instigator of a transpersonal ideal, the kingdom of God on earth, which is the ultimate purpose of the process of human evolution. If he did not periodically shake us from our fixed, unconscious lifestyle patterns of thought, attitude and action, our development would be even slower. Uranus emanates ideas of revolution into the minds of men, disturbing, fascinating, attractive visions which begin to obsess the minds of those capable of response, so that they begin the attempt at remaking the world to fit that image which is held in mind. Some call this the 'Divine Plan' that is seeking expression through transnational affinitive groups within humanity.

The first step in creating a world reflective of that holistic image is the firm belief that it is possible; the first step in re-creating our own lives is the belief that we do have the power and choice to do so, that we are free to change. We have already considered techniques which are transformative, and which reflect the creative process employed on a loftier scale by Uranus, and it is through such techniques of using the mind, imagination and visualisation that life can become magical again, as well as being reformed to fit us more comfortably. The Great Work confronting us is a personal and world transformation, so that life becomes ever more satisfying, enjoyable and fulfilling for as many as possible.

The spiritual self seeks not pain but well-being, and intends to transform life into a more pleasurable experience, and not the living hell that it is for many in today's world.

We need also to gain a more extended panoramic viewpoint of life, which, whilst not wasting time, also sees that, in the collective mind and the physical world, change often appears to occur very slowly. A historical perspective can reveal changes occurring that are not so obvious to the perception of the contemporary observer. Revolutionary ideas – especially those of such high ideals as Uranus – do take a long time to show real signs of achievement. The idea impresses itself on the collective mind, which then registers its presence, reformulates it into an ideal that is comprehensible in terms of current understanding and knowledge, and then releases it through an affinitive group to clash with the existing pattern. Reaction and opposition then occur, as there is a fight for supremacy between the old and new patterns, until, through a process of adaptation and integration, the new idea is absorbed into the mental climate, a transformation takes place, and as a result of a merging of old and new, something new emerges. We have seen this process in the French, American and Russian revolutions, none of which have yet embodied the founding ideals, and which, like the planetary New Age vision are still to be achieved in the future. Such broad changes take longer than a lifetime to manifest; whatever we may achieve in our lives will be seeds for the harvest of future generations to reap, just as we have enjoyed the benefits of achievements made by our forefathers.

Through us, a new approach is being made by Uranus to Gaia, the Sky God is returning to the Earth Goddess. Whilst mythologically, Uranus was castrated by Kronos–Saturn, and his power usurped, it was only an 'Age'. The creative inspirational spirit can never really lose his power, except as a part of an overall process that requires the withdrawal of that potency whilst more involutionary factors are necessary. The rebirth of Uranus in the human consciousness since the late eighteenth century is the sign of his re-emergence into activity; the clocks of a cosmic evolutionary transit have reached the appointed time. Gaia awaits the embrace of the Sky God, to awaken and initiate life on earth into a planetary consciousness. Within ourselves, the unification of body-mind-soul is the meeting place of this embrace. It is our responsibility to allow father-mother and god-goddess to merge. Through us, the new humanity can be born; evolutionary progress can be made as a result of the revolutionary spirit of Uranus.

Index